The Reagan Revolution: A Very Short Introduction

Very Short Introductions available now:

Available soon:

For more information visit our web site
www.oup.co.uk/general/vsi/

Gil Troy

THE REAGAN REVOLUTION

A Very Short Introduction

OXFORD
UNIVERSITY PRESS

OXFORD
UNIVERSITY PRESS

Oxford University Press, Inc., publishes works that further
Oxford University's objective of excellence
in research, scholarship, and education.

Oxford New York
Auckland Cape Town Dar es Salaam Hong Kong Karachi
Kuala Lumpur Madrid Melbourne Mexico City Nairobi
New Delhi Shanghai Taipei Toronto

With offices in
Argentina Austria Brazil Chile Czech Republic France Greece
Guatemala Hungary Italy Japan Poland Portugal Singapore
South Korea Switzerland Thailand Turkey Ukraine Vietnam

Published by Oxford University Press, Inc.
198 Madison Avenue, New York, NY 10016

www.oup.com

Oxford is a registered trademark of Oxford University Press

Library of Congress Cataloging-in-Publication Data
Troy, Gil.
The Reagan revolution: a very short introduction / Gil Troy.
p. cm.
Includes bibliographical references and index.
ISBN 978-0-19-531710-7 (pbk.)
1. Reagan, Ronald—Political and social views.
2. Reagan, Ronald—Influence.
3. United States—Politics and government—1981-1989.
4. Political culture—United States—History—20th century.
5. United States—Foreign relations—1981-1989.   I. Title.
E877.2.T767 2009
973.927092—dc22
2009002082

1 3 5 7 9 8 6 4 2

Printed in Great Britain
by Ashford Colour Press Ltd., Gosport, Hants.
on acid-free paper

Contents

List of illustrations

All photographs courtesy of Ronald Reagan Presidential Library, Simi Valley, California

Preface

"They called it the Reagan revolution," Ronald Reagan noted in his farewell address. "Well, I'll accept that, but for me it always seemed more like the great rediscovery, a rediscovery of our values and our common sense." Today, more than two decades after that 1989 speech, debate continues over just how revolutionary those Reagan years were. While most conservatives reject any criticism of their hero, an articulate minority laments that he did not go far enough. And while some liberals mourn just how much Reagan changed—and ruined—America, others mock him as a disengaged, do-nothing dunce. Nevertheless, Reagan's legacy continues to shape American politics, diplomacy, culture, and economics. Presidents Bill Clinton, George W. Bush, and Barack Obama all looked to Reagan's model of presidential leadership. On Monday, January 14, 2008, in Reno, Nevada, during the Democratic primary campaign, Obama said that Reagan "changed the trajectory of America in a way that . . . Richard Nixon did not and in a way that Bill Clinton did not." Meanwhile, many of the 1980s' debates about the budget, tax cutting, defense spending, and American values persist. Love him or hate him, Ronald Reagan remains the most influential president since Franklin D. Roosevelt.

In May 2007 the Ronald Reagan Presidential Library in Simi Valley, California, hosted the first debate for the ten Republicans

1. President Ronald Reagan running for re-election, October, 1984.

running for president in 2008. The moderator, Chris Matthews, opened the debate by noting that a recent poll had found that only 22 percent of respondents believed "this country is on the right track." Matthews then asked the candidates, "How do we get back to Ronald Reagan's 'morning in America'?" Eight months later, Senator Barack Obama complimented Reagan—prompting a fierce reaction from his primary rival Senator Hillary Clinton, who treated Obama's respect for Reagan's leadership style as endorsements of Reagan's program.

More than a quarter of a century after Ronald Reagan's 1981 inauguration, more than a decade after he withdrew from public view, and years after his death, Ronald Reagan seemed to be one of America's most popular politicians. In the 1980s, Chris Matthews was a former speechwriter for President Jimmy Carter, whom Reagan defeated for the presidency, working for Ronald Reagan's new nemesis, Speaker of the House Thomas "Tip" O'Neill. That Matthews, speaking in shorthand, could invoke Ronald Reagan's 1984 re-election slogan as a political gold standard was incredible. Even more extraordinary was how frequently the

Republican candidates mentioned Reagan during the campaign, virtually ignoring the unpopular Republican incumbent George W. Bush and Reagan's oft-neglected immediate successor President George H. W. Bush.

George W. Bush had experienced his own turnaround regarding Reagan. The intensely competitive junior Bush supported his father, George H. W. Bush, during the bitter 1980 contest for the Republican nomination, which Reagan won. The younger Bush then smoldered as both his parents suffered various slights from 1981 through 1989 during the elder Bush's tenure as Reagan's vice president.

By January 1989, the new president George H. W. Bush distanced himself from his predecessor, as Ronald Reagan retired to California. Bush emphasized that he was the real Reagan, with a model family, true heroics during World War II, and a regular habit of attending church, not just talking about it. Bush also emphasized that he was a hands-on chief executive, implying that Reagan was lazy and sloppy. The discussion in the Bush White House about Reagan became so contemptuous that former President Richard Nixon chided Bush's chief of staff, John Sununu. President Bush quickly phoned President Reagan to apologize.

Throughout the early 1990s, Ronald Reagan's historical stock plummeted. More people seemed to remember his gaffes not his gains, his losses not his wins. Debacles including the Iran-Contra scandal, $200 billion worth of savings and loan bankruptcies, and the $2.8 trillion budget deficit by 1989 tainted Reagan's legacy. Popular perceptions of Ronald Reagan focused on his hands-off, seemingly negligent management style; his buffoonish reliance on an astrologer for scheduling; his preference for sweeping rhetoric over constructive action. Ronald Reagan risked becoming a punch line, the rigid ideologue who thought trees caused more air pollution than cars, the aging leader who

snoozed when meeting the pope and once greeted his only
African American cabinet member at a conference of mayors as
"Mr. Mayor." When Bill Clinton, a young, relatively unknown
Arkansas governor, launched a long-shot bid for the presidency
in 1991, he and his wife, Hillary Rodham, condemned the greed,
selfishness, and empty political postures of the glitzy, heartless,
Reaganite 1980s.

Ironically, the Democratic victory in 1992 helped resurrect Ronald
Reagan's historical reputation. Bill Clinton's presidency triggered
nostalgia for Reagan's. The Democrats' embrace of the booming
1990s made it harder to criticize Reagan Republicans for
championing the booming 1980s. Bill Clinton's moral sloppiness
fed a yearning for an old-fashioned leader who never took off his
suit jacket in the Oval Office. And the end of the Cold War loomed
ever larger as an achievement, as the 1990s' economic growth
minimized the significance of the once formidable Reagan-era
budget deficits. At the same time, Ronald Reagan's classy letter
retiring from public life before Alzheimer's disease destroyed
his mind, and Nancy Reagan's devotion to her ailing husband,
boosted their popular and historical standing. As Ronald
Reagan's memory faded, memories of his presidency became
more vivid and positive.

Increasingly, even those who had detested him began to respect
him. Americans began realizing that he had been a consequential
president, for better and worse. The release of Reagan's speeches
from the 1970s and his presidential diaries showed he was no
marionette. He had a quick wit, a silver tongue, and a sunny
vision. Defining a taxpayer as "someone who works for the
federal government but doesn't have to take a civil-service exam"
turned his harsh critique of big government into easy listening.
Unlike his more thin-skinned successors, Reagan
adeptly defused criticism and puffed himself up with seemingly
self-deprecating gibes. Swatting away attacks that he was old,
lazy, and sleeping on the job, he insisted: "I have left orders to be

awakened at any time in case of national emergency—even if I'm in a cabinet meeting."

Reagan's revolution, restoration, and rediscovery continued to shape the country. Americans were living in a Reaganized America. America had emerged as the world's only superpower, enjoying a capitalist resurgence at home and abroad. Reagan's Sun Belt conservatism continued to shine—or cast a shadow, depending on one's perspective—in the courts, the Congress, and state capitals. In Washington, presidential power continued to grow, and congressional standing flagged, especially as Congress became more polarized. The Republican Party's liberal wing remained moribund and conservatives dominated. The quest to restore America's values and soul persisted, as did the blurring of popular and political culture. Prime-time television shows modeled themselves on White House life and created fictional presidents more popular than the actual incumbents, as stars such as California's Governor Arnold Schwarzenegger and the comedian Al Franken followed Reagan's path from showbiz to politics. Meanwhile, presidents and their wives played the fame game like Hollywood celebrities. Simple, visionary doctrines such as George W. Bush's war on terrorism and Barack Obama's "Yes We Can" sloganeering galvanized most Americans—at least momentarily—while alienating an articulate, passionate minority.

The fall 2008 financial meltdown triggered intense arguments about the new economy rooted in Reagan's 1980s. Americans debated whether the economic crash originated with Reagan-tinged trends such as the growth in service jobs rather than manufacturing, the conspicuous consumption, the ever-more abstract financial instruments, the media fawning over moguls, the regulatory rollback, and the growing gap separating the richest from the poorest. Yet even as experts pronounced the end of an era, Americans continued battling over many of the issues that launched Reagan's career: abortion, affirmative action, Social Security, taxes. Fortunately, the fights were tempered by the sentimental patriotism that he helped revive, as evidenced by America's resolve during the Gulf War, the country's unity-in-pain after September 11, the surge of enthusiasm in 2008 for Barack Obama's siren song of hope, and the Reaganite glitz-and-kitsch that punctuated America's annual calendar, from Super Bowl Sunday in January to the mass Christmas shopping spree in December.

With each passing year, it became clearer that Ronald Reagan's greatest achievement was in reviving—and transforming—American nationalism. Ronald Reagan was a romantic, aw-shucks, all-American patriot. His rise in politics was fueled by the backlash against the sixties' countercultural radicalism and self-criticism, which degenerated into the seventies' defeatism and pessimism. Reagan revived Americans' traditional self-confidence, restoring their optimism about their country's future. His unabashed, often-teary-eyed and tear-inducing patriotism was choreographed by his handlers but heartfelt on his part. His red-white-and-blue Technicolor nationalism suited the television age. Moreover, rather than rejecting many of the sixties' most important reforms, from civil rights to women's liberation, he helped mainstream them, producing what we can call the Reagan Reconciliation.

Reagan's patriotism was guilt-free, a decadent nationalism soothing a consumerist superpower that lacked nineteenth-century America's thrift or humility and had lost faith in many mid-twentieth century big government programs. With Ronald Reagan's mix of feel-good rhetoric and surprisingly cautious domestic policies, Americans could succumb to the broad appeal of a communal vision, without inconveniencing themselves individually. Reagan found vindication in what we can call his three P's—patriotism, prosperity, and peace. The result was a revolution that, like life, was complex and occasionally paradoxical. It was more incremental than extensive, producing a conservatism that was more modern than revanchist, led by a nimble politician who was more moderate than fanatic and more effective but less dominant than supporters hoped and opponents feared.

This Very Short Introduction to the Reagan Revolution focuses on some of the critical questions that still fill the historical agenda regarding Ronald Reagan and his era. This thematic approach required occasional departures from strict chronology but tries to explain how the Reagan Revolution, such as it was, developed over time and how it continues to resonate today. The constraints of space prevent me from specifying the many friends, colleagues, research assistants, web gurus, friends, and relatives who have helped me study Reagan and his Revolution for more than a decade, and especially all those who helped me with *Morning in America: How Ronald Reagan Invented the 1980s*, which Princeton University Press published in 2005. But I would be remiss if I did not single out my brother, Dr. Tevi Troy; Oxford's superb, originally anonymous reader, Professor Alonzo Hamby; and the McGill honors and graduate students in my "Reagan and the 1980s" Seminar of 2008–2009, for reading an earlier draft so thoughtfully; Merav Fima, Bonnie Goodman, Michelle Shain, and Anav Silverman for exemplary research and Web support; the talented archivists at the Ronald Reagan Presidential Library in Simi Valley, California, and the Thomas P. O'Neill Papers, John J. Burns Library, Boston College, in Brookline, Massachusetts, the History Department and Faculty of Arts at McGill University in Montreal, Canada, along with my welcoming new colleagues at the Bipartisan Policy Center in Washington, DC; my superb editor, Susan Ferber, along with the entire crackerjack Oxford University Press team; and my amazing wife and four wonderful children for indulging me as I have continued living in the 1980s well into the twenty-first century.

Chapter 1
Was Reagan a dummy?

Like heat-seeking missiles, the gibes mocking Ronald Reagan's intelligence pursued him as a president and still dog his historical reputation. The Washington wise man Clark Clifford dismissed Reagan as an "amiable dunce." The historian Garry Wills called Reagan "Mr. Magoo," after the bumbling cartoon character who stumbled repeatedly because he stubbornly ignored his bad vision. Garry Trudeau's *Doonesbury* comic strips depicted Reagan's brain as unduly aggressive, minimally analytic, and overstuffed with "images of an idyllic America," including "5-cent Cokes, Burma Shave signs, and hard-working White people." These characterizations of Reagan the dummy are entertaining but wrong.

Ronald Reagan was a savvy, ambitious, idea-driven politician who frequently appeared unthreatening, naïve, unintellectual, and apolitical. He had people smarts more than book smarts. He was more intuitive than analytical, more impressionistic than precise, more of a big picture visionary than a rigorous detail man. But he loved facts and ideas, even if he occasionally twisted his storehouse of facts and anecdotes to serve his ideology and punctuate his parables. So, yes, the old Hollywood hand could tell the prime minister of Israel that he had visited the Nazi concentration camps, when he had seen them on film.

And he could frustrate aides and journalists with inaccurate claims about how many thousands of hours General Motors lawyers' devoted to filling out government forms, or who was cheating as a "welfare queen." But most Americans forgave these lapses as an enthusiast's exaggerations rather than the fumbles of a fool.

Reagan enjoyed being underestimated. During the campaign for California's governorship in 1966, the incumbent Edmund G. (Pat) Brown dismissed Reagan, a political rookie, as a mere actor. Fourteen years later, in the 1980 presidential race, the incumbent Jimmy Carter and most White House aides derided Reagan as a doddering fanatic. "The American people are not going to elect a seventy-year-old, right-wing, ex-movie actor to be president," Carter's right-hand man, Hamilton Jordan sneered. Reagan won both elections.

Ronald Reagan was a great political showman and an ideologue. Opponents consistently attacked him inconsistently, as both clueless and fanatic, leading many Americans to reject both slurs. Reagan's Hollywood celebrity and Mr. Nice Guy amiability smoothed his ideological rough edges. To meet Reagan, to listen to one of the many radio talks he gave during the 1970s, to hear the presidential addresses he delivered so effectively, was to realize that he was a man with a mission, a believer in a conservative revolution and the American dream. He redeemed Americans' faith in their own country as what the Puritan John Winthrop called the "shining city upon a hill."

Ronald Wilson Reagan's complicated, often misleading, lifelong game with the world stemmed from his experiences growing up in the Midwest, the region he fled in his twenties but deified his whole life. Born in a small apartment in Tampico, Illinois, population 820, on February 6, 1911, Reagan spent his childhood hiding from the ugly realities of life with an alcoholic shoe salesman father, Jack Reagan. "Our family didn't exactly come from the wrong side of the tracks," Reagan would claim, "but we were certainly always within sound of the train whistles." His mother, Nelle Wilson Reagan, was a calmer, more reassuring presence, whose deep faith in the pacifist, individualistic Protestant Disciples of Christ denomination, today also known as the Christian Church, further set her son apart from his peers.

Naturally charming, Reagan learned to pretend to be an insider despite being an outsider. Like many of his contemporaries, he would remember being poor, but not really knowing it. But unlike many, he sought refuge in the conventional because of his unconventional upbringing—resulting in an individualist who outwardly appeared to be the ultimate conformist. His feelings of inadequacy—and fears of being exposed—fuelled his ambition along with an appealing but idiosyncratic romantic, self-dramatizing streak. Typically, he adjusted his name to fit his self-image, preferring the more "red-blooded," all-American nickname "Dutch" to "Ronald."

Bouncing around small-town northern Illinois in the 1910s and 1920s, tired of making new friends, and embarrassed by his family's circumstances, young Reagan withdrew into his Victorian mother's world, the world of books. From his mother, Reagan also learned how to become some of the heroes he read about, if only temporarily. One night, Nelle Reagan had her youngest son deliver a short speech as part of a staged reading she organized in these days before movies, radio, and television saturated America. For an insecure, lonely child craving approval, the clapping and laughing proved addictive.

After moving five times in less than a decade, the Reagans settled in Dixon, a town of 10,000, one hundred miles west of Chicago, when Reagan was nine. One cold, winter night two years later in 1922, Reagan found his father passed out in the snow near the front door. Reagan recalled wanting to leave his father outside. But knowing his small town's prying eyes and wagging tongues, he feared the neighbors would hear his father's loud snoring and snicker, humiliating the entire family. Reluctantly, resentfully, he dragged his father inside and put him to bed. Following his family protocols, he never told his mother.

Severe nearsightedness further insulated young Reagan. Not until he was thirteen or fourteen did he accidentally don his mother's glasses and discover that the world was not full of blurry "blobs." Lost in his own world but sensitive to his surroundings, Dutch Reagan became a solitary people person. Despite being a loner, he learned how to charm a crowd. This paradox would lead to a Hollywood celebrity who was universally liked but never fully accepted, a Hollywood "square" with an independent streak, producing a president famous for being likable but surprisingly inaccessible. Even Nancy, his devoted wife, would compare him to a brick wall.

Loving to be liked, Reagan pursued drama, sports, and student politics, three arenas where he could play the hero despite his family background. In 1926 the fifteen-year-old Reagan became a lifeguard. Further sensitizing Dutch to the dangers of being lulled by illusions, a lush, seemingly placid, riverbend in Dixon's Lowell Park hid powerful undercurrents. Over the next seven summers Reagan saved seventy-seven swimmers flailing in Rock River's deadly currents. He took great pride in that statistic, yet most of the swimmers resented his help. At home and in Lowell Park, Reagan learned that "people hated to be saved."

Dutch Reagan wavered between carefree optimism and deep despair: "I wonder what it's all about, and why / We suffer so, when little things go wrong?" he wrote in one high school poem. "We make our life a struggle / When life should be a song." The optimism for which Ronald Reagan became famous was achieved at great effort and only by ignoring surrounding turmoil and internal anguish.

Reagan attended Eureka College, a small, co-educational, Disciples of Christ institution near home. Sustained by a "Needy Student Scholarship" and odd jobs, Reagan thrived. Tall, charming, and handsome, the economics major was a BMOC, a big man on campus. He earned passable grades while winning letters in three sports and serving as basketball cheerleader, yearbook features editor, and student body president. "Going to college offered me the chance to play football for four more years," he would quip. Reagan also won a national acting contest. Knowing better than to admit such a fey ambition publicly, by senior year Reagan secretly dreamed of becoming an actor.

Reagan graduated from Eureka in 1932 with his optimism intact despite the Great Depression blighting America. "Oh, it was a small town, a small school, with small doings," he would recall. "It was in a poor time without money, without ceremony, with pleasant thoughts of the past to balance fears of the uncertain future." He had learned to be an actor, on stage and on the street. He took pride in being a savior, whether people wanted it or not. And he delighted in being cheerful, understanding that people flocked to buoyant, confident types and did not want to hear about anybody's pain, no matter how lonely, embarrassed, marginal, or forlorn they might feel.

Eureka shaped Reagan socially and psychologically more than it defined him ideologically and intellectually. He emerged as a consummate gentleman and a self-contained sort, apparently sunny and open, in fact emotionally distant and closed. As Ronald Reagan entered the "real world," his intellectual journey began in earnest. From the 1930s through the 1950s he mastered the showmanship, developed the commitment to free enterprise, learned the love of liberty, and internalized the hatred of Communism that would shape his presidency.

Maturing in the 1930s, disappointed in his own father, Ronald Reagan worshiped President Franklin D. Roosevelt with a filial devotion. Reagan remained personally grateful that a New Deal program employed his father. More broadly, he saw how the president restored hope and moved the nation with "fireside" radio chats, inspiring speeches, bold programs, wit, and warmth. Like so many sons disappointed in their fathers, Reagan would spend his life collecting heroes. These heroes seized his imagination and sculpted his vision rather than filling the emotional void that remained. Reagan's devotion to Franklin Roosevelt was such that, in later years, he denounced the Democratic Party, big government, high taxes, the Great Society, the bureaucracy the New Deal created, but not FDR.

Shortly after graduating college, Reagan became a radio sports announcer in Iowa, first in Davenport, then moving to Des Moines in April 1933. With the fluidity of a jazz maestro improvising riffs, Reagan brought to life curt, telegraphic wire service summaries of games. He secured the job by calling an imaginary football game on the air and making it sound compelling. Reagan combined his love of performance and his love of sports on this magic carpet of the imagination—at $100 a month during the depth of the Depression.

In 1937, while covering the Chicago Cubs' spring training camp in Southern California, the twenty-six-year-old sports announcer took a screen test. His agent described him as a "likeable, clean-cut American" type, especially appealing to young girls and older women. Warner Brothers' movie studio offered him a seven-year, $200-a-week contract. Dutch Reagan packed his 1934 Nash Lafayette convertible coupe and moved west.

Ronald Reagan quickly felt at home in the land of illusions. Hollywood's masters of make-believe restyled his hair, tailored his shirts to make his head and shoulders appear better proportioned, and sought a new name for Dutch Reagan. The new arrival sold his handlers on his real name.

A good boy without being a prig, Reagan lived modestly. He soon rented an apartment in West Hollywood for his mother and father, whom he would support for the rest of their lives. Reagan often accompanied his mother to church and supported her many charities. He was hardworking and reliable, far less extravagant and self-absorbed than most actors. "I'm a plain guy," he wrote in one movie magazine, still trying to conform. "I'm interested in politics and governmental problems. . . . Mr. Norm is my alias, or shouldn't I admit it?"

Reagan played the "good guy" if not always the hero. In fifty-three films from 1937 until 1964 he only played one villain. Starting, as most contract players did, with B movies, he was soon calling himself the "Poor Man's Errol Flynn," handsome enough to be a swashbuckler, not quite charismatic enough to be a star.

In 1938 Reagan met the beautiful blonde actress Jane Wyman. She was divorcing her first husband and far too saucy for a "square" like Reagan. Wyman first doubted "that a man could have so even a disposition consistently." She soon learned this was "the real Ronnie," optimistic, affable, dependable, honorable, and steady.

Ronald Reagan and Jane Wyman married in 1940. Hollywood expected a fairy-tale marriage. Reagan told his volatile, insecure bride: "We'll lead an ideal life if you'll just avoid doing one thing: Don't think." Within a year Jane had given birth to a daughter, Maureen, and the Reagans were saving up for a new home, a seven-room hilltop house overlooking Hollywood that was "not a mansion" and within their means.

In 1940 Reagan lobbied intensely to star as one of his heroes, the college football legend George Gipp in *Knute Rockne: All American*. When Reagan, playing George Gipp on his deathbed, muttered the eternal words, "win one for the Gipper," he further immortalized Gipp while launching his own transformation into a national icon.

2. Ronald Reagan as "the Gipper," George Gipp, in the film *Knute Rockne—All American*, 1940.

The bombing of Pearl Harbor derailed Reagan's movie career and, ultimately, his marriage. Reagan spent World War II helping to produce four hundred training films for the U.S. Army as Jane's career began to blossom. Captain Reagan's wartime service further steeped him in the red-white-and-blue patriotism of his youth, while honing his abilities to mass-produce effective messages.

After three-and-a-half years of stateside duty, Reagan began asking "Where's the rest of me?" echoing the line he used when starring in his other great film, *Kings Row*, as a double amputee. He wanted to flee "the monastery of movies." He plunged into politics, becoming involved in the Screen Actors Guild (SAG).

The SAG was a bourgeois union representing the entire range of actors, from Hollywood's royalty to obscure bit players. Always able to earn his peers' trust, Reagan quickly worked his way up, serving as president from 1947 to 1952—then again from 1959 to 1960. He enjoyed managing the internal conflicts and the broader struggles with studio heads as Hollywood reeled from bitter strikes and unnerving changes. Recalling his union experiences—and his years working in Hollywood's studio system—Reagan would say that tough studio bosses like Jack Warner taught him how to negotiate.

Reagan also followed current events more intensively than ever, infuriated by the government's growing intrusion into daily life. In the years after World War II, Reagan soured on the heavy-handedness of Roosevelt's New Deal and Harry Truman's follow-up, the Fair Deal. He remained a Democrat, endorsing the liberal, anti-Communist group founded in 1947, Americans for Democratic Action, and supporting Truman's election campaign in 1948. Still, Reagan saw his own incentive to act in additional films dwindle as taxation rates hit 90 percent, once he had earned a certain salary. As SAG president, he resented the bureaucratic regulations strangling his industry and others.

Reagan and the rest of Hollywood also felt the dizzying shift from fighting fascism to fighting Communism. A committed minority of radicals hoped to reach the masses through the cinema. Overreacting against a real threat, anti-Communists in Washington exaggerated the impact of Hollywood's colony of Communists, using it to feed the broader Red Scare. From his

California close-up, Reagan saw a band of ruthless radical schemers trying to hijack his industry.

Learning to expose Communist fronts, Reagan had enough unpleasant brushes with violent Communists that, at one point, the police advised him to pack a pistol. When he defended Franklin Roosevelt's son Jimmy at a meeting of supposed liberals that turned out to be full of Communists, Reagan found himself denounced as a "fascist," "a Red-baiter," an "enemy of the proletariat." These experiences made anti-Communism Reagan's defining political stance. "How do you tell a Communist? Well, it's someone who reads Marx and Lenin," Reagan would gibe. "And how do you tell an anti-Communist? It's someone who *understands* Marx and Lenin." Reagan detested liberal appeasement. He would proudly report the former Communist Sterling Hayden's explanation for why Communists failed to subvert Hollywood: "We ran into a one-man battalion named Ronnie Reagan."

While this new engagement in union business and national politics renewed Reagan, Jane Wyman plunged into more demanding acting roles. Reagan's political passion and speechifying bored her. "If you ask Ronnie what time it is, he tells you how to make the watch," she said, dismissing her long-winded husband.

Trying to reconcile without disrupting Jane's career, the Reagans had adopted a baby boy, Michael, in April 1945. Consigned to a nanny, Michael did little to bring his alienated parents together. In December 1947, Jane abruptly told reporters she was divorcing her husband. Although he tried to avoid the topic of his failed marriage, when pressed, Reagan blamed his ex-wife. "I *was* divorced in the sense that the decision was made by someone else," he explained, emphasizing his passivity.

Just weeks before the unhappy personal news, in October 1947, Reagan told the House Un-American Activities Committee about

Communist influence in Hollywood. Reagan's testimony infuriated liberals who resented the Red-hunters' zealotry. Yet before Congress, Reagan was temperate. He dismissed the Communists as a "small clique" and defended democracy as the best vehicle for exposing "their lies." Revealing the populism that would become his political marker, Reagan echoed Thomas Jefferson's claim that "if all the American people know all of the facts they will never make a mistake."

A month later, Reagan was elected to a full term as president of the Screen Actors Guild, having already filled the role temporarily for months. Still, Reagan drifted, devastated by the divorce, acting occasionally in roles that usually bored him. He first met Nancy Davis in 1949 during this period of despair—and debauchery. Nancy had been identified in the *Hollywood Reporter* as a "known Communist sympathizer." The director Mervyn LeRoy interceded on her behalf with the SAG president. Reagan discovered she was confused with another Nancy Davis. LeRoy prodded him to call Nancy and explain the mix-up over dinner. Each claimed to have an early casting call, in case the date was a dud. They stayed out until 3 a.m.

Just as Ronald Reagan's emotional detachment and rich fantasy life marked him as a child of an alcoholic, many of Nancy Davis's behaviors marked her as a child of divorce. Her parents split shortly after her birth in 1921. She, too, learned early in life to respond to adversity with fantasy. But unlike Reagan, she had a heavier touch. Her dissimulations often appeared dishonest; his seemed delightful.

Born as Anne Frances Robbins, Nancy took on the last name "Davis" years after her peripatetic actress mother Edith Luckett finally settled down and married a prominent Chicago doctor, Loyal Davis. In Chicago, Nancy blossomed from the chubby daughter of a scandalous Bohemian mother to a poised debutante with acting aspirations. Nancy dressed impeccably at

Smith College, mastering the masquerade. Having worked hard to reinvent herself, Nancy Davis clung to the conventions, the clothing, to protect her from her past as she built her own acting career.

Nancy Davis loved the very qualities in Ronald Reagan that Jane Wyman despised. Nancy claimed that "one of the things I liked about Ronnie right away was that he didn't talk only about himself . . . his world was not limited to himself or his career." The two transplanted midwesterners also shared a common desire to have an old-fashioned family life, even though he was a thirty-eight-year-old divorcé and she—at twenty-eight when they met—already was deemed an "old maid." Los Angeles would prove to be a fitting venue for these two rootless individuals trying to maintain appearances.

After a prolonged, rocky courtship, on March 4, 1952, Ronald Reagan and Nancy Davis finally married in a small ceremony witnessed only by their actor friends William and Arden Holden. Seven-and-a-half months later, on October 22, 1952, Nancy gave birth to Patti, a fully formed, seven-pound daughter. "Go ahead and count," Nancy declared in 1989, after enduring years of speculation that she forced Reagan's hand.

"From the start, our marriage was like an adolescent's dream of what a marriage should be," Ronald Reagan would say, acknowledging that dreams were their yardsticks. Alas, the family the two created, with Patti, and then Ronald Prescott Reagan, born in 1958, lacked the warmth, stability, and values the Reagans publicly embodied. Patti would portray her mother as cold, compulsive, and abusive. Nancy Reagan would admit that she loved her children, but she did not always like them. All four Reagan children suffered as the bond between Ronnie and Nancy became so intense it eclipsed all others, including their various offspring. In the 1980s, when the Librarian of Congress, Daniel Boorstin, would praise the Reagans' exceptional "love and devotion," President Reagan responded, "if Nancy Davis hadn't come along when she did, I would have lost my soul."

During the early years of the marriage, Reagan's movie career—which still provided most of his income—sputtered. Prosperity returned in 1954, when he began hosting CBS's weekly *General Electric Theater*. Reagan soon became GE's public face, regularly visiting its 135 plants across the country to praise the company's world of tomorrow. "Although he wasn't running for any political office, essentially he spent eight years campaigning," Nancy would explain, "going out and talking to people, listening to their problems, and developing his own ideas about how to solve them." Putting his great wit and easy charm to good use, Reagan honed his message, perfected his smooth speaking style, and coined many one-liners against Communists and against government agencies, which he said could out-compete private companies by being "tax-free, rent-free and dividend free."

Ronald and Nancy Reagan became icons of America's great prosperity, as the postwar boom swept millions of the Depression's abandoned daughters and impoverished sons into gleaming new homes and traditional roles. During the Kennedy years, Nancy mimicked Jackie Kennedy's style. Ronald Reagan was less impressed with Jackie's husband, John Kennedy, having joined Democrats for Nixon in 1960. While touring GE factories, Reagan was becoming more hostile to the Democratic Party and the social welfare state. His increasingly conservative rhetoric unnerved his corporate bosses, prompting the TV show's cancellation in 1962.

Critics caricaturing Ronnie as an empty vessel would claim the ambitious Nancy and her archconservative stepfather, Loyal Davis, transformed Ronald Reagan, the amiable New Dealer, into a conservative crusader. While Dr. Davis offered moral and financial support, Reagan's political obsessions predated his marriage. Nancy simply supported her husband. "If Ronnie were selling shoes, I'd be out pushing shoes," she would say.

Reagan would attribute his political conversion to the lure of "the mashed potato circuit," the many banquet speeches that kept aging actors busy. Addressing Americans who were not in show business, he warned that the overtaxation and smothering regulation afflicting Hollywood would soon plague them. Increasingly, businessmen swarmed him saying, "Let me tell you what's *already* happening to our industry!" After one speaking trip, Reagan recalled, he told his wife: "Look, you know it's just occurred to me that I go out and make all these speeches of things that I'm against and then I go out and campaign for the Democrats who are making it happen. I'm going to stop."

"Maybe my party changed. I didn't," Reagan insisted. Years later, he explained his conversion to the Republican Party by saying, "I was a Democrat when the Democratic Party stood for state rights, local autonomy, economy in government, and individual freedom. Today it is the party that has changed, openly declaring for centralized federal power and government-sponsored redistribution of the individual's earnings."

In middle age, Reagan still was finding new heroes, especially conservatives who fleshed out his anti-Communist and capitalist instincts. Having always had to work for a living, he admired his independently wealthy friends. *Witness*, Whittaker Chambers' 1952 manifesto denouncing "godless" Communism and lily-livered liberalism, transfixed Reagan. Dusting off his undergraduate economics degree, Reagan started reading the classical capitalist economists. He particularly liked Frederick Hayek's *Road to Serfdom*. Reagan was an early follower of William F. Buckley and his fellow firebrands in the conservative insurgency's weekly bible, the *National Review*. Appalled by taxes and Communists, entranced by these visionary thinkers, Reagan's own Republican conservatism became more coherent and compelling.

The national political limelight began shining on Ronald Reagan with his speech, "A Time for Choosing," urging Barry Goldwater's election in 1964. Reagan recycled lines he had perfected over years of haranguing hapless listeners about big government on Hollywood sets, in nightclubs, at his home. Reagan wanted America to fit a traditional vision as ardently as he wanted his family life to realize the small-town ideal. Months after Goldwater's debacle, forty-one wealthy businessmen established "The Friends of Ronald Reagan." Reagan entered the California gubernatorial race in January 1966 with a recognition factor of 97 percent. He had finally found "the rest of me" he had sought since World War II.

Reagan felt he was making a selfless sacrifice in entering politics. Still, cynics snickered that only in California would a washed-up B movie actor with no political experience run for governor. In one Democratic advertisement the incumbent governor Pat Brown would tell a black student: "I'm running against an actor. And you know it was an actor who shot Lincoln, don't you?"

Ronald Reagan would make a career out of being underestimated. "He's a lot sharper than people give him credit for being," one aide told *Newsweek*. In November 1966, Reagan won by nearly one million votes in a state where Democrats outnumbered Republicans almost five to three.

Reagan's conservatism saved him from being just a handsome Hollywood type. His role as what the actor James Cagney called "the zealous defender of the American dream" anchored his political career and insulated him from charges that he lacked substance. Supporters hailed him as "the symbol of all the great American virtues: honesty, fortitude, courage, strength and humility." Reagan's detractors alternated between dismissing him as an inexperienced actor and caricaturing him as a right-wing lunatic. The attack on his politics gave him credibility, just as his good looks, sunny approach, and Hollywood background made his ideology appear more palatable. Reporters and other intellectuals attacked Reagan's lack of "sophistication," not realizing it was his Jimmy Stewart down-to-earth qualities that made him popular.

Reagan offered Goldwater's conservatism with a smile rather than a grimace. Governor Reagan was as capable of celebrating the *Peanuts* comic strip with "Happiness-Is-Having-Charles Schultz-as-a-California-Resident day" as he was of denouncing the welfare state. "Ronnie improves the stodgy image of the Republican party," one *Esquire* profile would concede. "He gets their message across with a sugar coating. You don't notice the castor oil in all that orange juice."

As governor, Ronald Reagan built a national reputation by combating the sixties' social and political revolutions. He defended America's war in Vietnam, questioned the civil rights revolution, opposed women's liberation, and confronted radical students. His enduring popularity in the state that many other Americans blamed for spawning such movements proves that Reagan, like Richard Nixon, shrewdly heard the "silent majority" amid the student protesters' din.

Reagan refused to be cowed. He was, however, willing to talk. He engaged his critics on all the issues, no matter how intimate. He defended "solid moral principles" wherever they were under attack, from boardrooms to bedrooms. When a young woman challenged his opposition to birth control and abortion, he answered her frankly. "I see the larger problem of trying to find a way to reverse the hedonism while at the same time having full compassion for those young people who in spite of all teaching are going to make mistakes," he wrote, perhaps remembering his own missteps. Reagan believed that deviations, no matter how widespread, did not invalidate long-standing "standards." He preferred a conception of "sin," even if violated, to its alternative—degenerating into "hedonism."

With the "personal" becoming so political—and political life getting so personal—the Reagan family endured intense scrutiny. As her father fought "the movement," their daughter Patti was swept up in it, and her betrayal enraged her mother. At home and in the office, Nancy was Ronald Reagan's enforcer. As he smiled, she glared. If many of his opponents found it difficult to dislike him personally, so many supporters disliked his wife. She balanced out his automatic trust in his subordinates and his passivity amid conflict. Nancy's passion occasionally seemed to intimidate Governor Reagan himself, but he learned to put it to good use.

Reagan's two terms as California's governor from 1967 to 1975 thrilled conservatives, despite his occasional compromises. Reagan was a big-picture politician, delegating details to subordinates. His quick wit, muscular stands, and delight in crossing swords with radicals made him a national celebrity. Inheriting a $200 million budget deficit, Reagan doubled corporate taxes while increasing the personal rate from 7 to 11 percent. Perhaps more surprisingly, he signed the Therapeutic Abortion Act in 1967 legalizing abortion when the mother's health was at risk. Reagan reversed his position three years later, after more than two million women used the liberally worded loopholes. Reagan challenged doctors who wanted more latitude: "Who might they be doing away with? Another Lincoln, or Beethoven, an Einstein or an Edison? Who shall play God?" In his second term, Reagan burnished his conservative credentials with a tough welfare reform bill that reduced the welfare case load by 300,000 within three years.

His opposition to "sixties liberals" defined his career. He was the conservative Kennedy, charismatic enough for the masses, ideological enough for the partisans and intellectuals. In 1968 many of the millionaires who had bankrolled his gubernatorial run encouraged a presidential run, but it fizzled. By 1975, with Nixon disgraced and Gerald Ford stumbling his way toward the political center, conservatives insisted that Reagan run for president.

Ronald Reagan suffered his first and only electoral loss in 1976. But he took heart in how close he had come to unseating an incumbent president. Reagan soon understood the unpleasant primary fight as a rehearsal for 1980, when Republicans would be poised to seize the White House from the increasingly unpopular incumbent president, Jimmy Carter.

Most observers believed that Jimmy Carter, a nuclear engineer, was smarter than Ronald Reagan, the actor. Since the 1930s, liberals often treated their adversaries condescendingly, assuming that anyone who disagreed with them must be intellectually or morally inferior. Since Franklin Roosevelt, Democrats and reporters have mocked the intelligence of every Republican president other than Richard Nixon. Dwight Eisenhower was supposedly a tongue-tied sloth preferring golfing to governing. Gerald Ford became a national joke, ridiculed as a klutz by *Saturday Night Live*'s comedian Chevy Chase, forever defined by Lyndon Johnson's cruel conjecture that Ford never recovered from playing football without a helmet. George H. W. Bush's tendency to get tongue-tied had many joking that he spoke English as a second language. This slur stuck to George W. Bush, too, broadening to include attacks on the junior Bush for being intellectually rigid, incurious, lazy, and shallow. Yet, Eisenhower was a shrewd general, now appreciated as a deft "Hidden Hand" president. Ford was a skier and Yale Law graduate. Both Bushes attended Yale, and in Bush junior's case, Harvard Business School.

Playing the populist card, presidents like George W. Bush and Ronald Reagan displayed a nonacademic intelligence, thriving as intuitive people-persons appearing as "regular" guys. In 1988 George H. W. Bush munched pork rinds to compensate for his moneyed pedigree. During the 2000 presidential contest, more Americans identified with George W. Bush's seemingly sincere tongue-tied expressions than with Al Gore's smooth sculpted paragraphs.

The 1980 election would demonstrate that the smarter person was not necessarily the better politician. And just because he was not a nuclear engineer, Ronald Reagan clearly was no dummy. During his years in Hollywood he had developed a thoughtful worldview, rooted in texts, validated by his experiences. Gibes about his intelligence said more about his opponents' prejudices than about Ronald Reagan's shortcomings.

Chapter 2

Do Americans like their government big—or small?

Late in the afternoon on Election Day, 1980, Ronald Reagan was showering when the phone rang. Nancy answered the phone, then excitedly called her husband. Dripping wet, with a towel wrapped around his waist, Ronald Reagan fielded a phone call from the president of the United States, Jimmy Carter, who conceded the election. The call surprised Reagan. Pollsters had predicted a long night of uncertainty—and a minimal victory margin. Moreover, Carter called before voting booths closed on the West Coast, prompting many voters to stay home. Democrats blamed some key losses on Carter's premature concession.

Reagan interpreted his victory as a call for revolution, repudiating more than four decades of big government combined with the post–Vietnam War problem of a too-soft foreign policy. Even though his popularity ratings were the lowest a president-elect received since polling began in the 1930s, he buttressed his claims of a conservative mandate by pointing to the twelve Senate seats the Republicans gained, giving Republicans control of one branch of the legislature for the first time since 1954. Grassroots conservative organizations, especially NCPAC, the National Conservative Political Action Committee, had targeted leading liberal lions such as Senators George McGovern, Frank Church, and Birch Bayh. All lost their re-election bids. In the three months between the early November elections and the president's late January inauguration, Reagan and his aides would talk so much about his "mandate" that reporters began hailing—and fearing—the "Reagan Revolution."

Actually, Reagan's mandate was illusory. The 1980 election was mostly an ABC election—voters wanted Anybody But Carter. Reagan's Electoral College vote of 489 to 49 magnified his bare majority of 50.7 percent of popular votes cast, with Carter receiving 41 percent and the Republican renegade John Anderson attracting 6.6 percent. Reagan transformed these ambiguous results into a mandate for change, proclaiming in his inauguration: "In this present crisis, government is not the solution to our problem, government *is* the problem." In rejecting the governing assumptions of most American domestic policy since the 1930s, especially Franklin Roosevelt's New Deal and Lyndon Johnson's Great Society, Reagan boldly called for revolution, despite his slim popular vote victory margin.

Reagan preached that "Man is not free unless government is limited." He believed the American people had deputized him to cut government regulation, cut government taxes, and cut government programs, while restoring American pride, boosting America's defenses, and confronting the Russians. True, the American people were fed up with the status quo. True, elements of Reagan's program proved popular. True, the Senate transformation suggested the change was broader than a quadrennial White House personnel shift. Yet Americans were not ready for the sweeping changes Reagan envisioned. Just as Reagan extended a modest victory into a major mandate, he tried expanding a growing recognition that the Great Society was hobbled by great failures into a broader repudiation of the American welfare state—and that far, Americans were not yet willing to go.

By 1980 Americans were ambivalent. They retained enough of their historic fear of executive power to dislike big government in the abstract. But after nearly fifty years of Franklin Roosevelt's New Deal and Harry Truman's Fair Deal, of John F. Kennedy's New Frontier and Lyndon Johnson's Great Society, Americans were addicted to many of the government programs that together made their government big, their tax bills high, their bureaucracy dense. Democrats miscalculated by overlooking the growing backlash against big government and that revolt's historic roots; Republicans risked erring by overstepping and eliminating essential programs that Americans took for granted.

When Ronald Reagan was born in 1911, America's federal government was still too small to be either *the* problem or *the* solution. The Progressive movement was laying the groundwork for what would become America's mid-twentieth-century welfare state. But Reagan was born into an American regime more scaled to the expectations of America's Founders when they established the Constitution in 1787 than it was to the government he would head as a seventy-year-old.

Although the American Revolution was far less radical than the French or Russian Revolutions, Americans did rebel against executive power. The Revolutionaries' experience with the king of England—and his colonial governors—soured a generation on strong, centralized government. The younger men of the Revolution who helped fight the war, such as Alexander Hamilton, appreciated the need for an effective government. They championed the new Constitution in 1787, replacing the Articles of Confederation that reflected the initial revolutionary commitment to keeping the national government weaker than the states, and the executive weaker than the legislature.

Still, the Constitution established a federal government expected to defer to "We the People" and "these United States," as the country first was called. This question of how vigorous the new federal government should be split George Washington's cabinet. Secretary of State Thomas Jefferson, having opposed executive power so eloquently in the Declaration of Independence, fresh from witnessing the French Revolution, led the charge with his friend James Madison against a strong government—and executive.

When Secretary of the Treasury Alexander Hamilton proposed a National Bank in 1791, Jefferson opposed this power grab by subtly misquoting the Constitution. Jefferson claimed the Tenth Amendment left "*all* powers" not delegated to the federal government with the states or the people. Actually, the Constitution reads "the" powers not "all" powers, preserving popular and state prerogatives, but less globally. Hamilton countered by stretching the "elastic clause," Article I, Section 8, authorizing the new Congress "to make all laws necessary and proper for carrying into execution" the powers granted to the Federal government.

This Hamilton-Jefferson divide defined the debate for more than a century. Jeffersonian liberals wanted limited government, romanticizing farmers as ideal citizens, and trusting self-sufficiency over any government patronage. Hamiltonian conservatives wanted a vigorous government to help America develop, trusting private-public partnerships to serve the economy and the citizenry.

In the 1830s and 1840s, once-wealthy patricians, many based in Boston, launched private humanitarian campaigns. Economically displaced by the Industrial Revolution's new wealth and harsh practices, politically displaced by Andrew Jackson's democratic revolution, these elites asserted their authority through doing good. They reformed prisons, fought child labor, fed the poor, agitated to free the slaves. Their reforms mostly emphasized private attempts over public policies, and state or local structures over national ones. In jump-starting the abolitionist movement, they helped trigger the Civil War, which expanded the government dramatically.

While saving the union, President Abraham Lincoln envisioned the nation united, effective and supreme over the states. After the Civil War, *these* United States became *the* United States. The often forgotten part of Abraham Lincoln's Republican Party agenda advocated helping farmers and laborers, using national power to improve individuals' quality of life.

During the Civil War, with the rise of a national currency called the greenback, a national debt, and national income taxes, American business leaders noticed that government involvement could restrict their growth as much as feed it. In what the political scientist Clinton Rossiter called "the Great Intellectual Train Robbery of American History," conservative business leaders hijacked Jeffersonian small government liberalism. Their "laissez-faire" doctrine suggested that government should step back and let corporations thrive. This hands-off policy expected poor Americans to fend for themselves—or get help from relatives, churches, or volunteers.

Three decades later, delivering his second inaugural address in March 1893, President Grover Cleveland championed the conservative view that government should avoid giving welfare. Small government prevented sloppiness, laziness, and corruption. Cleveland echoed Jefferson's rigid reading of the Constitution's "necessary and proper clause." "Frugality among the people," Cleveland proclaimed, is "the best guaranty" of "free institutions."

Cleveland defined his lean, mean approach so sharply because it was under assault. The still-declining descendants of the Boston-based reformers still sought solutions to the crime, grime, poverty, and prostitution festering in the cities, as millions of exotic immigrants entered. Upholding the "Maternal Commonwealth's" domestic values in the public sphere to protect their private spheres, many middle-class women also demanded reforms. Viewing the family as "the miniature state," these women governed their children firmly while demanding that society reinforce those values.

The Populist movement of the 1870s, 1880s, and 1890s channeled an even stronger popular push for more governmental activism. Reacting to midwestern and southern farmers' misery, fueled by silver-mining interests who wanted a currency based on silver as well as gold, Populism demanded a government serving the people, not corporations. With the first billion-dollar company, U.S. Steel, forming, facing the plutocratic robber barons, Populists sought to use democracy to check big business. "We believe that the power of government—in other words, of the people—should be expanded . . . as rapidly and as far as the good sense of an intelligent people and the teachings of experience shall justify, to the end that oppression, injustice, and poverty shall eventually cease in the land," the Populist Party platform of 1892 stated. Even without winning much power, the Populists sowed many political and economic seeds, which sprouted into lasting reforms.

Progressivism, a more urban-based movement seeking order in industrializing America, helped implement many Populist proposals. Progressives included crusading social workers such as Jane Addams, career-oriented muckraking journalists such as Lincoln Steffens, and legislative reformers such as Robert M. LaFollette. Two presidents embraced Progressive ideas. Theodore Roosevelt, who served from 1901 through 1909, believed the president represented the plain people. Roosevelt deployed the presidential bully pulpit and government power to counterbalance corporate power. Radicalized after leaving the White House, in 1910 Roosevelt articulated a New Nationalism valuing "the national need before sectional or personal advantage." Roosevelt regarded the president "as the steward of the public welfare." His New Nationalist vision demanded judges "interested primarily in human welfare rather than in property," along with a Congress and state legislatures that "represent all the people rather than any one class or section of the people."

Roosevelt's successor, William Howard Taft, the president when Ronald Reagan was born, did little to advance Progressivism. On paper, Taft's successor, Woodrow Wilson, was even more radical than Roosevelt, and as much of a presidential superman. Whereas Roosevelt's New Nationalism endorsed big government eclipsing big business, Wilson's New Freedom wanted decentralized government and small businesses. In practice, Wilson's administration continued the Progressive trend of expanding federal power to assist individuals.

Historians often caricature the 1920s as a time of conservative backlash against Progressivism. The Progressive movement slowed down, the presidents were more passive, but many Progressive policies became institutionalized. Calvin Coolidge's secretary of commerce, Herbert Hoover, was a Progressive activist. Americans loved Hoover as "The Great Humanitarian" who ran massive relief projects in Europe after the Great War and in Mississippi after the great flood of 1927. Hoover trusted rational negotiation and representative government commissions to smooth capitalism's rough edges by setting standards, even adjusting prices. When the stock market crashed in 1929 with Hoover serving as president, he tried using government power to defeat the ensuing Depression. But Hoover underestimated the emergency. Explaining his incremental approach in his starchy way made him look more hidebound than he was.

Still, the Great Depression of the 1930s initially highlighted Progressivism's limits—and Americans' continuing allergy to big government. Business interests protecting private property invoked Thomas Jefferson's small government liberalism to reject government redistribution and regulation as anti-American. The despair spreading through society, combined with the hopes radicals in Europe and Soviet Russia generated, challenged

American stability and values. While only a few actually waved the banner of revolution, many feared that America's economic system was broken, and America's sclerotic political system made it unfixable.

In those dark days, Franklin D. Roosevelt's infectious optimism brightened America's mood, while recalibrating American ideology. Roosevelt's "First Hundred Days" in office set a template of presidential action and established precedents for direct government intervention. Mixing Jefferson's democratic populism with Hamilton's top-down centralization, Roosevelt created big government liberalism. "I am not for a return to the definition of liberty under which for many years a free people were gradually regimented into the service" of capitalism, Roosevelt said. Liberalism "is plain English for a changed concept of the duty and responsibility of government toward economic life."

Appealing to the collective conscience, justifying emergency actions with military analogies, Roosevelt offered a three-pronged program. First, he mobilized governmental power to offer immediate *relief*, shifting the responsibility from churches, community groups, and relatives to the local, state, and federal governments. Then, he tried jump-starting a *recovery*, putting the government in the business of micromanaging the economy—and violating the long-standing American aversion to federal budget deficits. Finally, he sought broader *reforms* to institutionalize the changes and prevent future disasters.

Suddenly, the president was choreographing currency shifts, bringing electricity to the South, eliminating corporate abuses, and subsidizing individual homeowners. The government provided the old with pensions, the disabled with support, and the poor with food while hiring millions through a new "alphabet soup" of agencies, the CCC (Civilian Conservation Corps), the PWA (Public Works Administration), the AAA (Agricultural Adjustment Administration), and the NRA (National Recovery

Administration). The "Blue Eagle" seal of approval on businesses upholding the NRA codes invited consumers to support companies treating labor fairly. These businesses could display their "badge of honor" as in wartime, Roosevelt said. He believed in "planning, communal cooperation, and government intervention in areas once off-limits." The "first duty of government is to protect the economic welfare of all the people in all sections and in all groups," Roosevelt said in a 1938 fireside chat. This casual statement departed from Alexander Hamilton's vision, let alone Thomas Jefferson's.

Roosevelt's "New Deal" did not end the Great Depression, but it reassured Americans. It repositioned the government and the president at the center of American political, economic, and cultural life. World War II jump-started the economy—and launched a half-century of unprecedented economic prosperity. America became the world's first mass middle-class society.

The war introduced much government intervention, regulation, and taxation that millions in 1932 would have deemed "Bolshevik." But step by step, improvisation by improvisation, speech by speech, and crisis by crisis, Roosevelt had brought Americans to a new vision. Europeans still criticized America's limited welfare state; Americans sensitive to history were surprised at how far this initially reluctant giant had moved toward government activism.

Roosevelt was a shrewd politician as well as a charismatic, visionary, and expansive national leader. He caricatured conservatives as greedy, selfish, Hooverite "economic royalists," who caused the Great Depression and neglected the "Forgotten Man" or woman. Roosevelt was nimble enough to woo Republicans when necessary, entering World War II with a bipartisan cabinet. Still, Roosevelt's onslaught defined and demoralized American conservatism for a generation.

After Harry Truman's Fair Deal expanded Roosevelt's program, the 1952 election (bringing the first Republican to power since Herbert Hoover) proved that the New Deal had instituted lasting changes. A moderate realist, Dwight Eisenhower respected America's domestic and foreign policy consensus. He explained to his brother Edgar, a doctrinaire conservative, that if any political party "attempt[ed] to abolish social security, unemployment insurance, and eliminate labor laws and farm programs, you would not hear of that party again in our political history." Two decades into the Roosevelt revolution, the number of those who rejected fundamental social welfare building blocks was "negligible and they are stupid," Eisenhower proclaimed.

By maintaining signature New Deal programs such as Social Security, Eisenhower ratified Roosevelt's vision and preserved America's new welfare state. Eisenhower also averted a bruising partisan battle. True, Eisenhower disappointed the Republican right. But after the Roosevelt-Truman onslaught, Eisenhower assessed conservatives' limited power accurately, if harshly. The popular liberal civil rights movement in the 1950s and Senator Joe McCarthy's demagogic right-wing anti-Communism helped further marginalize conservatives, who increasingly seemed to be on the wrong side of history, and of the American sensibility.

Some voices on the Right revived. Ayn Rand's two blockbuster odes to individualism, *The Fountainhead* (1943) and *Atlas Shrugged* (1957), became ideological road maps for millions. In founding the *National Review* in 1955, the young Yalie William F. Buckley began steering conservatism away from what he called "Crackpot Alley." Buckley criticized big government without the anti-Semitism and racism that characterized the "John Birchers" and many of the New Deal's harshest foes. Ronald Reagan's own conservative awakening stemmed from the anti-Communism he shared with Hollywood buddies such as Charlton Heston channeled into a broader frustration with big government.

The federal government's meteoric growth and the equally rapid emergence of a national focus enabled the civil rights movement of the 1950s and 1960s to succeed as a national movement fighting an injustice rooted most intensely in one region, the South. The civil rights movement's success in an age of big government and national television furthered the development of a national conversation about once local problems—and the search for national solutions. John Kennedy's tragically brief presidency raised expectations further.

Increasingly, the debate during Kennedy's years was no longer "should the federal government be involved?" but "how should the federal government solve particular problems?" What was so revolutionary about this shift was that it no longer seemed remarkable. Government had become so big, so centralized, and so central in Americans' lives that many forgot how novel a phenomenon the welfare state was in American history. It would take Ronald Reagan nearly twenty years of speechifying to remind Americans that questioning big government was not marginal or anti-American, but rooted in America's political tradition. It seemed that Americans liked their government small in the abstract, but big when it came to helping them.

Chapter 3

Was there a call for a Reagan revolution (or what happened to the Great Society)?

In the early 1960s, Americans became more collectively self-critical, aware of those who were left behind even as the baby boom and the economic boom boosted American self-confidence. In 1962, Michael Harrington's explosive exposé of poverty, *The Other America*, sensitized Americans to 40 million fellow citizens living below the poverty line, including 28.3 million whites. Three decades after Franklin Roosevelt's election, amid a great boom not a Great Depression, Harrington and others described an ingrained culture of poverty, furious that the poorest Americans, comprising 20 percent of the population, received only 5 percent of the national income.

Other critics chronicled crises in health care, housing, education, and the environment. In 1965 only 14 percent of children from families with incomes less than $3000 attended nursery schools. In 1960, 38 percent of high school students failed to graduate. Eight million Americans, more than Michigan's entire population, had not finished five years of school. And too many classrooms were overcrowded, with curricula outdated, teachers underpaid.

Lyndon Johnson became president in 1963 trusting in a governmental solution for nearly every American problem.

"The roots of hate are poverty and disease and illiteracy, and they are broad in the land," Johnson proclaimed in an early speech, planning to legislate these scourges into oblivion. Johnson linked the challenges of Communism, civil rights, and poverty. He wanted to win the Cold War by perfecting America, vindicating democracy worldwide.

In May 1964, Johnson redefined America's historic mission at the University of Michigan's commencement ceremonies. After settling the land, Americans developed an industrialized infrastructure. During this next stage Americans would go beyond mere riches and power, "to enrich and elevate our national life, and to advance the quality of our American civilization." Johnson envisioned a "Great Society," providing "abundance and liberty for all. It demands an end to poverty and racial injustice.... The 'Great Society' is a place where every child can find knowledge to enrich his mind and to enlarge his talents.... It is a place where the city of man serves not only the needs of the body and the demands of commerce but the desire for beauty and the hunger for community."

To implement his radical vision, Johnson had to win the 1964 election. After a bitter primary battle, the Republicans nominated Senator Barry Goldwater to oppose Johnson. Back in 1960, Goldwater had published a blockbuster manifesto, *The Conscience of a Conservative*, that eventually sold more than 3.5 million copies. Goldwater defended the Jeffersonian idea that the government that governs best, governs least. Like William F. Buckley, Goldwater tried to avoid the cranks and the haters. But some of Goldwater's attacks on sacred cows like Social Security backfired, as did his famous proclamation: "Extremism in the defense of liberty is no vice. And moderation in the pursuit of justice is no virtue." Democrats distorted Goldwater's statement of principle into the ravings of a fanatic.

Lyndon Johnson caricatured Goldwater as an extremist who would trigger war with the Soviets while eliminating three decades of liberal progress at home. Johnson triumphed, winning 43.1 million votes to Goldwater's 27.2 million votes, 61.1 percent to 38.5 percent. The Democrats also gained two Senate seats and 37 House seats, solidifying their control over both Houses of Congress.

In retrospect, Goldwater's 27 million votes compared favorably to the 31 million vote total for Hubert Humphrey in 1968 and the 29 million votes George McGovern would earn in 1972. Moreover, 3.9 million Americans volunteered for Goldwater, revealing impressive grassroots support. The New Deal had worked too well. The Roosevelt Democrats, once alienated ethnics and overburdened laborers, were becoming middle-class suburbanites. As they prospered and moved from the cities, their politics changed. Goldwater's losing campaign introduced some important actors whose compelling messages would revive conservatism while recruiting these "Reagan Democrats" of the future.

Ronald Reagan's blockbuster speech for Goldwater in the campaign's closing weeks, "A Time for Choosing," was the most important premier. Having recently become a Republican, Reagan campaigned vigorously for Goldwater, whom he knew through his in-laws. After one triumphal fund-raiser at Los Angeles's legendary Coconut Grove nightclub, Republican bigwigs decided that Reagan's speech should be broadcast nationally. With the actor John Wayne's help, the Republicans purchased half an hour on NBC-TV. Goldwater's advisers tried cancelling the broadcast, fearing Reagan's attacks on Social Security abuses would backfire. Goldwater viewed the tape—which Reagan insisted on recording before the kind of live audience he had been wooing for years—and barked: "What the hell's wrong with that?"

3. Ronald Reagan giving a speech supporting Senator Barry Goldwater for president in Los Angeles, 1964; Goldwater is to Reagan's right.

In what became known as "The Speech," Reagan attacked decades of government centralization, appeasement of Communism, and impingement on freedom. Speaking in his honey-smooth affable style, oozing great faith in America, Reagan left viewers feeling optimistic even when he criticized. Reagan pitched the question of the election as "Whether we believe in our capacity for self-government or whether we abandon the American Revolution and confess that a little intellectual elite in a far-distant capital can plan our lives for us better than we can plan them ourselves?"

The choice, Reagan claimed, was not between left or right but "up or down—up to man's age-old dream, the ultimate in individual freedom consistent with law and order—or down to the ant heap [of] totalitarianism." Channeling Franklin Roosevelt and Abraham Lincoln, Reagan proclaimed: "You and I have a rendezvous with destiny. We will preserve for our children this, the last best hope of man on Earth, or we will sentence them to take the last step into a thousand years of darkness."

Reagan went to sleep that night worried his speech had failed. At midnight, a Goldwater staffer called from Washington, where it was 3 a.m. The aide reported that the campaign switchboard was still alight with fund-raising calls the speech had generated. Republicans replayed the speech repeatedly, helping to launch Reagan's political career, despite Goldwater's humiliating loss.

Propelled by the landslide, Lyndon Johnson surpassed the New Deal. In 1964 and 1965, Johnson muscled through an ambitious array of laws that transformed the way the government helped the poor, the sick, the old, the young. Eventually, staffers counted 207 laws as "landmark" legislative achievements. Under Johnson, the federal budget first topped $100 billion. Aid to the poor nearly doubled, health programs tripled, and education programs quadrupled. The permanent civil service expanded from 1 million strong when Eisenhower retired in 1961 to 1.3 million federal workers eight years later.

Alas, Johnson could not legislate away America's problems. Even as Congress passed a landmark civil rights law, the Voting Rights Act, riots erupted in Watts, the Los Angeles ghetto. The Vietnam War, which Johnson tried pinning on Goldwater in 1964, became Johnson's albatross—and America's burden, wasting billions of dollars, sacrificing 50,000 American lives, and bleeding away America's credibility and confidence. Johnson's Great Society hopes sank in the Vietnam morass; he retired prematurely, refusing to run for re-election in 1968.

Johnson's successor, Richard Nixon, a Republican, proved equally ineffectual amid ever-sobering challenges. The sixties protest movements continued generating a sense of social unrest and failure after such high hopes. The economy, which purred nicely in the 1960s, imploded; building a Great Society while fighting a war broke the bank. Under Nixon, America also endured escalating oil prices, producing a great inflation linked with rising unemployment called stagflation. And amid all these crises, Richard Nixon's Watergate crimes destroyed his presidency, shattering Americans' confidence in their leaders, their institutions, and themselves.

Richard Nixon's tenure also disappointed conservatives. But the effect was paradoxical. Nixon's acceptance of many Great Society initiatives the Democratic Congress advanced, from environmentalism to affirmative action, and his "détente," accommodation, with the Soviet Union and Communist China, demoralized conservatives. Ultimately, however, Nixon's "betrayal" emboldened conservatives to confront the Republican establishment. The Republican Party would soon stop welcoming everyone into its "big tent" and become more right wing.

Increasingly, Ronald Reagan became the voice of American conservatism. Although he served honorably in the Senate, Barry Goldwater never recovered his national standing after his 1964 defeat. William F. Buckley remained the elitist intellectual voice and prickly conscience. Reagan was the movement's everyman, the gentlemanly political leader with a twinkle in his eye to balance the anger, but able to summon the wrath of the prophets when necessary.

As governor of California from 1967 to 1975, a job that included overseeing the University of California system, Reagan enjoyed confronting radicals. He dismissed hippies as people who "dress like Tarzan, have hair like Jane, and smell like Cheetah." More seriously, on May 15, 1969, he authorized a police raid against protesters occupying People's Park in Berkeley, California, the legendary center of sixties radicalism. The violence reinforced his reputation as a conservative tough guy—even though he compromised on other key conservative principles, including signing the 1967 bill allowing abortions if necessary for the mother's well-being.

Reagan reinforced his foreign policy credentials by focusing attention on the Vietnam POWS and their families' misery. Once out of office, he would become détente's leading critic. Later in the decade, he opposed ratifying Jimmy Carter's treaty returning the Panama Canal to Panamanian sovereignty.

Reagan remained in the national spotlight by delivering short radio commentaries and speaking throughout the country. His topics reveal the ideological building blocks of the conservative revolution that was gaining momentum. He targeted unreasonable bureaucrats, criminal-friendly judges, welfare cheats, spoiled college students, appeasement-minded liberals, soft-headed liberals, narrow-minded liberals. He—and others—claimed that, thanks to the Great Society's failures, Franklin Roosevelt's noble experiment to help starving Americans in the 1930s metastasized into a government gargantuanism and Bolshevik collectivism squelching American individualism.

As he quipped his way around the country, Reagan started weaving together the disparate strands of American conservatism. When he worried that détente is "what a farmer has with his turkey—until Thanksgiving day," he articulated the anti-Communists' fears. McCarthyism's excesses had undermined the anti-Communist movement's credibility.

A new generation of anti-Communists arose in the 1970s, unblemished by the 1950s' Red-baiting. Many called themselves neoconservatives, lapsed liberals appalled by the New Left's post-sixties' excesses, infuriated by the crime epidemic, and terrified of the surge in Soviet aggression following America's Vietnam humiliation.

When Reagan joked about government not solving problems but subsidizing them or defined taxpayers as people who work for government despite never taking a civil service exam, he was playing to Goldwater's supporters. These libertarians demanded small decentralized government to preserve American freedom and revive America's economy. This instinctive call—rooted in the Framers' fear of overweening government—resonated with a new breed of economists and legislative reformers, who blamed the Great Society's overreach for the nation's economic stagnation. Some "Supply Siders" made the counterintuitive claim that cutting taxes actually raised government revenues, because more money in tax-paying citizens' pockets ultimately overflowed into government coffers. Other activists focused on trimming government expenditures to reduce the budget deficit.

And when Reagan proclaimed: "If we ever forget that we are One Nation under God, then we will be a nation gone under," social conservatives cheered. These traditionalists opposed the sixties' cultural excesses, and particularly abhorred the Supreme Court's 1973 *Roe v. Wade* decision legalizing abortion. The abortion fight—and American culture's broader drift toward secularism, sensuality, and cynicism—galvanized a growing network of religious leaders, particularly Evangelical Protestants. Self-described pro-family, pro-life, pro-religion lobbying groups, especially the Reverend Jerry Falwell's Moral Majority, would help spur a religious revival and a political mobilization. As a result, some analysts labeled this period the "Fourth Great Awakening," the latest wave of the spiritual and political convulsions that rocked America periodically since the 1730s.

These sometimes overlapping, sometimes clashing, conservative ideologies found new audiences after the 1960s. The traditional conservative alliance of Main Street sensibilities and Chamber of Commerce business interests needed reinforcing. Sun Belt suburbanites—fiscally conservative and social moderate consumerist pioneers who followed the good weather to Florida and Texas, Arizona, and California—joined with Rust Belt urbanites, solid middle-class and working-class types feeling hounded by high taxes, increasing crime, and forced school integration by busing children to segregated schools. The parents of these "Reagan Democrats" had been the backbone of Franklin D. Roosevelt's coalition.

Gradually, a network of organizations and periodicals grew to sustain conservatives and deliver them from their wilderness years. Organizations such as the YAF, Young Americans for Freedom, began positioning alumni all over Washington. Magazines such as William F. Buckley's *National Review* were more integrated into the capital's culture. Think tanks such as the American Enterprise Institute and the Heritage Foundation produced a burgeoning catalogue of conservative solutions to contemporary problems. These foundations would be to this new generation of conservatives what Harvard and Yale had been to the New Deal and New Frontier liberals—both intellectual hothouse and meal ticket.

Conservative policy solutions also gained momentum, from budget-cutting talk in Congress to the tax-cutting moves reflected in the popularity of the Kemp-Roth 30 percent tax cut, the faith in "Supply Side economics," and grassroots campaigns to roll back property taxes by referenda that succeeded in California and Massachusetts. In March 1980, the Texas Democrat Phil Gramm and the Michigan Republican David Stockman launched their congressional "Bipartisan Coalition for Fiscal Responsibility." They proposed $38 billion in budget cuts to justify the Kemp-Roth tax cuts.

Even though the 96th Congress never cut the budget, the Gramm-Stockman plan marked a milestone in American political life. This rough draft of Reagan's economic manifesto appeared nearly a year before Ronald Reagan's inauguration, and independent of the Californian. Gramm and Stockman also had a dry run in trying to pass what would be the Reagan budget. Their bipartisan coalition included "old guard" Republicans like Bob Michel, "young Turks" like Newt Gingrich, and conservative Democratic "Boll Weevils" like Kent Hance, all of whom would help pass the Reagan budgets.

The national discourse had changed abruptly. "It was a new market, a new era—the era of budget subtraction," Stockman later exulted. "For the first time since the New Deal, everyone was talking about cutting the budget instead of adding to it."

Beyond Congress, foot soldiers educated and energized by Moral Majority churches and New Right direct-mail appeals furthered conservatism's ideological, institutional, and intellectual renaissance. While hand-wringing liberals fretted about "Why Americans Hate Politics," conservatives churned out one best-selling manifesto after another, be it Milton and Rose Friedman's pro-capitalist *Free to Choose* (1980), George Gilder's pro-growth *Wealth and Poverty* (1981), Charles Murray's anti-welfare state *Losing Ground* (1984), or Allan Bloom's moralistic *The Closing of the American Mind* (1987). These controversial books spurred debate and changed the American ideological universe.

Only parts of this conservative critique gained traction in the American mainstream. More and more Americans felt harassed by onerous government regulations, depressed by the nation's drift, scared of street crime, worried about the economic dislocations, frustrated by the new limits on energy, American power, and American aspirations but at the same time outraged by the concessions to minorities, which only seemed to intensify minority demands and anger. More Americans endorsed the conservative explanation for the nation's dysfunctions. Yet the overwhelming majority still accepted the fundamental assumptions of the New Deal and the Great Society. Americans remained Franklin D. Roosevelt's children, believing in big government, trusting the president and the federal government to help them and their neighbors if necessary. Yes, most Americans still shared an internalized, ancestral ambivalence about big government, which conservatives successfully reawakened. But few considered turning back the clock to the days of Herbert Hoover.

Still, Americans were unnerved. By the 1970s, the rebellious antics once attributed to marginal East Coast or West Coast hippies had conquered the heartland. Society's floodgates opened, unleashing the sexual revolution, the backlash against authority, the culture of questioning. The *Roe v. Wade* decision legalizing abortion triggered the Culture Wars. Subversive cultural touchstones from *The Godfather* to *The Exorcist* undermined traditional faith in the family, the church, sex roles, and the world's linearity, especially given the political and economic traumas. The counterculture found the mass market as jeans, granola, marijuana, and rock 'n' roll became multibillion-dollar industries. Crew cuts and suits were for squares; sideburns and bell bottoms were cool. Millions found their life plans detoured by drugs, divorce, sexual promiscuity, and selfishness, buffeted by unwelcome power struggles pitting husbands against wives, children against parents. Marijuana use among high school seniors peaked in 1978. High school yearbooks showed many young men with long hair in 1978, not 1968.

Americans seemed strangely unable to cope with their brave new world. The crime wave, which began in the 1960s, made many Americans cower when they left their homes, losing faith in the government's ability to protect them—and in liberalism's promise of salvation. The Great Society bogged down in bureaucracy, generating taxes and regulations but not social justice. Détente appeared futile, as the Soviet Union appeared increasingly menacing. Amid all the leisure, the liberation, the toys, the cries to "Let the Sun Shine In," these were dark days. Many Americans despaired as families imploded and communities exploded.

Nations need good faith and a common spirit as glues to stick together and work together. The 1970s witnessed a multidimensional crisis of American nationalism. With the collective vision blurring, many questioned the notion of a common good. Americans lost faith in their country, their institutions, their leaders, their neighbors, and themselves. Political scientists described Washington's "Iron Triangle" of congressional committees, federal bureaucrats, and special interest lobbying groups, sacrificing the national good for particular agendas. Harvard professor Samuel Huntington feared that America's democratization in the 1960s may have undermined its "governability."

While becoming increasingly self-centered, many Americans also began championing subgroup special interests. John Kennedy's call to open American life and opportunity to all had degenerated into what the journalist Theodore White condemned as "an attempt to peg citizens into categories by race, sex, and ethnic heritage." The government was busing students by race, instituting bilingual education for immigrants, counting Americans—for the first time—by ethnic group in the census, and imposing racial and gender quotas in corporations and universities. White feared a balkanized America: "In trying to eradicate racism, the politics of the sixties and seventies had institutionalized it."

Americans talked incessantly about rights, rarely about responsibilities. The activist Supreme Court became the champion rights-granter, plunging into volatile issues affecting religion, education, housing, even conceptions of life and death. Instead of trusting legislators to compromise or presidents to lead, judges decreed. The Court's decision legalizing abortion in 1973 was so controversial partially because it was so abrupt and sweeping. The many court rulings to integrate schools by busing children to neighborhoods far from home were so controversial because they micromanaged intimate parental and local decisions without the expected, popular democratic input.

Americans' tough choices in the 1970s fed nostalgia for the 1950s' good old simple days. Busing lacked the moral clarity of outlawing segregation; abortion fights complicated the push for women's rights; affirmative action allowed whites to feel resentful. But President Kennedy and the Reverend Martin Luther King Jr. had taught how to make expanding civil rights about improving America, using the language of Christianity, the Declaration of Independence, and Cold War patriotism. Americans needed another effective leader to guide them out of the dark cave of special-interest selfishness into the centrist sunshine where they could feel confident enough to perceive happiness, stability, and liberty as collective accomplishments and communal adventures, not personal assets or selfish journeys.

Conservative dismay with Richard Nixon and his moderate successor Gerald Ford prompted Reagan's run against President Ford for the 1976 Republican nomination. This primary battle violated what Reagan himself had frequently invoked, the Republicans' "Eleventh Commandment." Coined during Reagan's 1966 gubernatorial primary race by a California Republican, the commandment proclaimed: "Thou Shalt Not Speak Ill of a Fellow Republican."

Reagan justified his challenge by emphasizing Ford's foreign policy failures. He accused Ford of abandoning a crucial ally in allowing South Vietnam's fall in 1975. Reagan also feared the Nixon-Ford détente policy appeased the recalcitrant Soviet Communists and weakened America.

Reagan's effective appeals—and a pivotal win in North Carolina—brought Republicans to their national convention without a nominee. At the convention, the party establishment secured President Ford's nomination. Conceding, Reagan gave a seemingly impromptu speech wondering what to write in a time capsule to be buried until America's tercentennial in 2076. Reagan lamented "the erosion of freedom that has taken place under Democratic rule in this country, the invasion of private rights, the controls and restrictions on the vitality of the great free economy that we enjoy." He warned about the threat of nuclear destruction. Then, he challenged the crowd, saying the readers of the future would know what happened. Reagan asked: "Will they look back with appreciation and say, 'Thank God for those people in 1976 who headed off that loss of freedom, who kept us now 100 years later free, who kept our world from nuclear destruction?'"

Cheers rocked the convention hall. Many observers predicted that the speech guaranteed Reagan's nomination four years later. After Ford lost to Jimmy Carter in the 1976 election, Reagan enjoyed a front-runner status—and a role as the leading Republican during the Carter years.

In upholding tradition, Reagan offered a politically potent contrast to the Democratic incumbent Jimmy Carter. As a candidate, Carter charmed many alienated baby boomers by quoting the folk singer Bob Dylan and wearing jeans, having internalized elements of the sixties critique along with the boomers' angst. As president, Carter angered many traditionalists by embracing the zeitgeist. Many Americans were not ready for a "Times They Are a-Changin'" president who wore a cardigan sweater, carried his own bags, and banned the playing of "Hail to the Chief."

Throughout Carter's administration, the economic crisis that began under Richard Nixon intensified. Carter's "misery index" from 1976, the combination of inflation and unemployment, nearly doubled in four years from 12.5 to over 20. In September 1980, the annual inflation rate of price increases hit 22.3 percent. The prime interest rate for lending money rose to 11.25 percent. As the inflation rate, the unemployment rate, and the divorce rate all soared, American confidence plummeted further.

Unfortunately, Carter failed to offer the leadership Americans craved. Carter squandered goodwill and power with his arrogance, amateurism, and half-measures. He seemed unable to whip inflation, manage the energy crisis, tame the media, or master foreign affairs, coming to embody American defeatism.

Carter reacted to the growing conservative critique by governing somewhat from the right. Zero-based budgeting, justifying every expense anew each year, reflected the backlash against the mushrooming national deficit. Deregulating the airlines, trucking, railroads, oil, and banking anticipated the Reagan revolution. And a defense buildup began reviving the military after the demoralizing retreat from Vietnam.

Still, Carter was buffeted by so much criticism, he frequently stumbled. Saying the search for energy independence was the "Moral Equivalent of War" allowed cynics to reduce this roar to its initials: MEOW. When Carter tried managing legislators, lobbyists, or labor unionists, he alienated them while critics claimed he indulged them. Too honest to instill confidence, in a *Sixty Minutes* television interview Carter gave himself only "a B" on leadership, "a B-minus" in foreign policy, and a "C" in domestic policy.

Carter tried exorcising Vietnam's ghosts and restoring America's foreign policy luster by championing human rights. Yet his administration faltered repeatedly overseas. The Soviets extended their tentacles in the Horn of Africa, Central America, and the Middle East, while the United States languished. Europeans criticized America for being too soft. Overcoming their dislike of dictators as long as they were anti-Communist, critics excoriated Carter for abandoning American allies, especially the Shah of Iran and Nicaragua's Anastasio Somoza. "A posture of continuous self-abasement and apology vis-à-vis the Third World is neither morally necessary nor politically appropriate...." the neoconservative political scientist, Professor Jeane Kirkpatrick, exclaimed in 1979. "Liberal idealism need not be identical with masochism, and need not be incompatible with the defeat of freedom and the national interest."

By June 1979, Carter was less popular than either Lyndon Johnson or Gerald Ford had been at their respective lows. Only 33 percent of Americans polled approved the president's performance. Increasingly, and characteristically for the times, experts questioned the presidency's viability and even doubted America's sustainability.

Many Americans also found Carter too critical of America and too self-critical. This discomfort culminated in July 1979, when Carter retreated to the presidential vacation compound, Camp David, for ten days. "I feel I have lost control of the government and the leadership of the people," Carter admitted at one of the many evaluation sessions he convened there to reassess his administration. The initiative became self-defeating "as soon as the White House staff decided to turn it into a public event," recalled Clark Clifford, one expert Carter invited. "Advertised to the world, it worsened the very problem it was designed to solve, conveying the sense that the President was confused and had lost confidence in both himself and the American people."

On national television, Carter discussed America's "crisis of confidence.... the growing doubt about the meaning of our own lives and ... the loss of a unity of purpose for our nation." He detailed the materialism, cynicism, pessimism, skepticism, apathy, alienation, and defeatism "threatening to destroy the social and the political fabric of America." Linking the ideas of progress, confidence, and national unity, Carter implicitly set up the 1970s as the reverse image of the 1950s. Although he never used the word, this became known as "the Malaise Speech." The address was searing, thoughtful, and self-critical. It was also ill-advised and self-destructive. Americans did not want a president preaching a gospel of doubt and negativity.

It was thus a weakened president in November 1979 who faced the crisis that killed his presidency, as Iranian radicals violated the American embassy's sanctity to kidnap diplomats and Marine guards. In an unhealthy symbiosis, reporters and the president created another hostage, the American people. The networks' daily tally of how long the crisis continued, combined with Carter's refusal to conduct normal business until the hostages were freed, enhanced the Islamic radicals' impact. The hostage crisis dragged out for 444 days, until Carter left office.

Most Americans demanded a military response immediately while Carter initially trusted diplomacy. The president in crisis seemed at once unsteady and too stubborn, too open to negotiate with the Iranians and too closed to alternative viewpoints. When he finally approved a military rescue attempt, it failed. When Secretary of State Cyrus Vance then resigned on principle, Carter was brittle and ungracious.

Six weeks after the hostage crisis began, the Soviets invaded Afghanistan. Feeling betrayed, after all his overtures toward Moscow, Carter overreacted. Politically autistic, misreading cues, Carter appeased when he needed to confront and bellowed when diplomacy might have helped. The Republican foreign policy guru Henry Kissinger sighed that the Carter administration had simultaneously alienated allies and adversaries, in both Europe and the Third World.

Carter's missteps set the scene for Reagan—but highlighted the ambiguities surrounding the new president's mandate. Reagan's smiley-face conservatism contrasted with Carter's sourness and Barry Goldwater's crankiness. Deploying his toastmaster skills, Reagan softened his harsh critique with quick quips. "Recession is when your neighbor loses his job. Depression is when you lose yours. And recovery is when Jimmy Carter loses his," Reagan gibed. His wit disarmed the Democrats, revealing a more agile mind than most people realized. Reagan also wrapped his proposals in the American flag, preferring to pitch a soothing restoration than an unsettling revolution. Reagan's crusade was not one of blood, sweat, or tears. It did not entail any new burdens. Reagan's crusade was one of joy, ease, and hope, to take government "off" Americans' "backs."

Secret Democratic policy memoranda warned of "a conservative strain . . . emanat[ing] from the voters—they perceive the federal government as spending too much—and in a wasteful manner." Some polls estimated two of three Americans demanded a balanced budget and reduced regulations. Democrats worried.

Nevertheless, conservatism's "happy warrior" and growing infrastructure could only do so much. Reagan and his supporters would claim they forged a cohesive conservative movement that retook America. In fact, it was more of a negative achievement— temporarily uniting a broad, frequently unruly, assortment of groups alienated from the Great Society, the Democratic Party, and the Carter Presidency. Congressman Mickey Edwards's lament from 1978 remained valid. Conservatives seemed unable "to consistently convert favorable public sentiment into legislative victories" or effectively "change or form public opinion."

Reagan proudly allied with the right, even as others wondered how to type him. Having been in politics for nearly two decades before running for president, Reagan understood politics as the art of the possible. He labeled his gubernatorial record conservative, explaining: "What is being called pragmatism is when I had some arguments with a very few conservatives. There are some people who think that you should, on principle, jump off the cliff with the flag flying if you can't get everything you want.... If I found when I was governor that I could not get 100 percent of what I asked for, I took 80 percent."

More seriously, Reagan had not convinced many he could cut taxes and boost defense spending without breaking the budget. The "Laffer curve," named after the economist Arthur Laffer, claimed that cutting taxes could generate more revenue by stimulating the economy. But this "Supply Side" theory was unproved, and Democrats estimated the tax cuts would lead to a $282 billion revenue loss and budget deficits as high as $30 billion. Even many corporate leaders, distrusting simplistic formulas, were "lukewarm" on Reagan, according to a *Fortune* survey.

While Reagan's economic policy seemed risky, many feared his foreign policy could destroy the world. "We believe that a Ronald Reagan victory increases the chances for nuclear war," the *Nation*'s editors warned. These qualms echoed Jimmy Carter's strategy to paint Reagan as a right-wing nut. To Carter and his allies, Reagan's nomination marked Barry Goldwater's second coming. Reagan's supposed stupidity and his extremism reinforced the stereotype. "He gives you so much ammunition," one Carter strategist exulted.

Reagan neutralized the assaults by appearing as reasonable as possible, trusting Carter's unpopularity to sway the election. During their one debate, on October 28, 1980, just days before the election, Reagan dispatched his opponent with one beautifully delivered line. Carter had just finished attacking Reagan for threatening to dismantle Social Security and abandoning sick Americans by opposing national health insurance. Carter had attacked at a rapid-fire pace, with a clipped tone, a pinched expression, and two lengthy sentences of more than 75 words apiece in his 250-word rebuttal. Reagan, in command, paused, looked over his shoulder at the president of the United States, smiled, crooked his head, crinkled his eyes, and nodded, saying, "There you go again." The crowd laughed. Reagan's poll ratings spiked. Gallup polls estimated that Carter's popularity plunged ten percentage points in the forty-eight hours before Election Day, one of the biggest drops ever recorded.

Reagan's Goldwater-conservatism-with-a-smile united disparate constituencies: Protestant evangelicals, infuriated by what they considered to be an immoral liberal minority's assault on American values, allied with blue-collar Catholics frustrated that the Great Society did not help them as the New Deal had helped their parents. Northeastern neoconservative intellectuals alienated by the counterculture and fearing Soviet expansionism found themselves working with southerners repudiating the Democratic Party's civil rights agenda. Corporate leaders dumbfounded by the Democratic addiction to big government and liberals' knee-jerk hostility to big business bonded with homeowners crushed by the double whammy of an eroding dollar and soaring property taxes along with Sun Belt residents rejecting high taxes and burdensome regulations. These constituencies first mobilized in the 1960s and 1970s and would galvanize conservatism in the 1980s and 1990s.

On Election Day, Reagan bested Carter in the South and the West, forecasting a new electoral coalition—what would be dubbed "Red America" in the twenty-first century. Reagan captured more than 40 percent of the normally Democratic union vote, as well as nearly half of the Roman Catholic vote, breathing life into a critical 1980s phenomenon, "the Reagan Democrat." Reagan's

4. Ronald Reagan and Jimmy Carter riding together to Reagan's inauguration, January 20, 1981.

share of self-identified Democrats' vote was 24 percent, an impressive figure that nearly constituted Reagan's entire victory margin. Carter's percentage of the Democratic vote dropped from 81 percent in 1976 to an estimated 66 percent. Reagan by contrast received 80 percent of the Republican vote—a mark of party discipline that would be the key to Reagan's strength with the electorate and in Congress. Middle-aged white males made up the heart of Reagan's constituency, with 53 percent of men and only 38 percent of women voting for Reagan, while 57 percent of whites and only 14 percent of blacks voted Republican.

Nevertheless, the victory appeared more definitive than it was. The electorate's volatility offered one hint. Voters' negativity offered another. More than half the voters said the choices were made based on "negative views of the candidates," the *New York Times* claimed. The referendum, such as it was, was more anti-Carter than pro-Reagan, making 1980 an "Anybody But Carter," election. One national poll estimated that nearly four of five Reagan voters supported him because of Carter's poor performance. "This wasn't a reluctant Ronald Reagan vote we were seeing," one politician insisted. "It was an enthusiastic anti-Carter vote."

The great conservative realignment of 1980 was chimerical. Only 28 percent of the electorate identified as "conservative," only 13 percent as strong Republicans, only one Reagan voter in ten identified Reagan's conservative ideology as a key motivator. Americans were not more conservative on questions of welfare, abortion, or the Equal Rights Amendment. Yes, voters wanted lower taxes and fewer regulations, but they still looked to government to solve social, political, and cultural problems. The historian Richard Wade bluntly concluded: "This is no big cosmic thing. Carter was a lousy President." And the Great Society had proved to be a major disappointment.

Chapter 4

Was there, in fact, a Reagan revolution?

On January 11, 1989, Ronald Reagan delivered his farewell address to the nation. Characteristically mixing personal modesty with patriotic grandeur, he rejected his nickname, "The Great Communicator." He explained: "I communicated great things, and they didn't spring full bloom from my brow, they came from the heart of a great nation—from our experience, our wisdom, and our belief in the principles that have guided us for two centuries." Further correcting the historical record, the president preferred labeling his era "the great rediscovery" rather than "the Reagan revolution."

Reagan celebrated two great recoveries: the economic recovery that produced nineteen million jobs and the morale boost that restored America as the world's leader. Still sensitive to the media pounding he endured, he insisted: "What they called 'radical' was really 'right.' What they called 'dangerous' was just 'desperately needed.'"

Ronald Reagan, the man who called the Soviet Union the "evil empire," rarely pulled punches rhetorically. He knew the "Reagan Revolution" label was catchier, more resonant, more historically flattering. Was this a final burst of modesty as the first president to complete two terms in office since Dwight Eisenhower retired?

Reagan's preference for "rediscovery" not "revolution" reflected a characteristic cautious streak, especially in domestic policies. It was not just that he liked rooting his actions in the rich soil of American history nurtured by enduring wellsprings of American values. He understood Americans' ambivalence about revolutions. Having rejected England with a conservative rebellion, Americans spent decades fighting the results of the Russian Revolution. It was particularly awkward for conservatives to pose as revolutionaries.

Reagan also knew that his governing approach had been more nuanced, more consensus-driven, less transformative than the grandiose title of "Reagan Revolution" implied. Reagan's administration was never as radical as he occasionally promised, conservatives desired, or liberals dreaded. Reagan offered more of a restoration than a revolution, more of a reorientation, shifting slightly toward a less liberal future than a repudiation of the past, including the Great Society. If historians judged the Reagan era on its most sweeping terms—or by the goals he and his most conservative supporters articulated—the Reagan Revolution was a dud. And if historians judged by the critics' fears—and doomsday warnings—about a return to back-alley abortions, mass hunger, institutionalized sexism, and the bad old days of Jim Crow, the Reagan Revolution also fizzled.

In more concrete terms, there were changes in the government's tone, the military's size, many federal judges' ideologies, America's approach to the world, especially the Soviet Union. In many critical areas, Reagan and the Republicans neutralized the government's decades-old role as regulator, enforcer, and to liberals, force for good, but to conservatives, obstacle to progress. Still, Reagan only slowed the government's growth rate; he did not stop the expansion. The federal budget, which was $590.9 billion in 1980 with $391 billion spent on domestic needs, was $2,655.4 billion in 2006, with $1,872.8 billion devoted to domestic needs. Under Reagan, the highest tax rates dropped dramatically, but the effective federal tax rates for all households were 22.2 percent in 1980, compared with 20.5 percent in 2005. Examining social issues, abortion remained legal in America, although the annual numbers dropped from 1,297,606 in 1980, meaning 25 per 1,000 women, to 830,577 in 2004, 16 per 1,000 women.

Thanks to the Reagan Reconciliation, the cultural revolution of the 1960s continued, despite Reagan's denunciations of New Left excesses. Warnings of a "backlash" against blacks, women, and gays were overstated, as was the caricature of Reagan as a racist, sexist, homophobe. The number of African American politicians nearly doubled from 5,038 in 1981 to 9,040 in 2000. The percentage of women politicians serving in House, Senate, and statewide offices more than doubled from 10.5 percent in 1981 to 24.1 percent in 2007. By 2008 a woman, Hillary Clinton, competed against an African American, Barack Obama, for the Democratic presidential nomination. And not only were millions of gays living comfortably out of the closet, gay marriages and civil unions were openly discussed and legalized in some states, marking a dramatic breakthrough.

What drove the Reagan Revolution and what limited it, or morphed it, into a "great rediscovery"? To understand this we need to appreciate the powerful inertia—and widespread popularity—of the post–New Deal dimensions of government, the peculiar dynamics of the 1980s, and Ronald Reagan's strengths and weaknesses as a leader.

For all the 1970s' political, economic, social, and cultural discontent, the United States remained remarkably stable. Despite the twentieth-century expansion of governmental and specifically presidential prerogatives, the president was no dictator. The Constitution carefully distributed power among the Congress, the courts, and the presidency on the federal level, while encouraging a tug-of-war between the states and the national government locally. These checks and balances limited the changes Reagan or any president could implement. Reagan's key aide in trimming the federal budget, the Office of Management and Budget's director David Stockman, would mourn the limits of presidential power. After watching his efforts to trigger a conservative revolution falter, Stockman complained that America's Constitution fragmented government power so much it prevented substantive reform.

Further frustrating radical conservatives was modern Americans' addiction to big government and the New Deal–Great Society status quo. Americans often opposed governmental goodies others received, while ignoring their own appetites. Business leaders grumbled about welfare abuses while blocking Stockman's proposals to cut corporate subsidies. Farmers muttered about all the money going into the ghettoes—without even purchasing social peace—while protecting anachronistic agricultural subsidies lingering from World War I.

Ultimately, most Americans acknowledged that, despite all the government's inefficiencies, America's big government also accomplished great things. By 1980, the half-trillion-dollar-a-year federal budget ate up nearly one-quarter of America's gross national product. Spending on all levels of government consumed 36 percent of the GNP. Beyond the military, more than one million federal government workers distributed billions of dollars in handouts to farmers and physicians, exporters and importers, small businessmen and major corporations. Dozens of federal agencies, from the United States Fish and Wildlife Service to the Office of Labor Management Standards, supervised, regulated, and micromanaged American life.

More and more Americans bristled as private businesses spent more than $100 billion responding to the flurry of bureaucratic regulations generating ten billion pieces of paper annually. The heroic New Dealers of the 1930s and the idealistic Great Society social activists of the 1960s now seemed to be replaced by the arrogant, out-of-touch federal bureaucrat. Many citizens resented working nearly half the year to pay the government, especially amid hyperinflation and steep interest rates. It became easy to believe the large federal budget deficits and burdensome federal regulations were strangling the economy.

Yet this insatiable Mr. Hyde, devouring hardworking Americans' tax dollars, was also a Dr. Jekyll feeding the hungry, housing the homeless, healing the sick. In 1980 one out of every two American households received some federal, state, or local government support, 37 million individuals accepted Social Security assistance, 50 million children attended 170,000 schools, and a quarter of a billion Americans enjoyed using 29,500 post offices, one million bridges, and four million miles of roads.

Nearly half a century after the New Deal, most Americans looked naturally to Washington to solve all problems. Even clear state or local questions regarding abortion, the death penalty, and crime frequently became national controversies. The Supreme Court's ever-expanding purview and the president's centrality in any political discussion nationalized these and other local issues.

Reagan continued his winning election strategy as president. That meant that from the start he frustrated conservatives. His preference for the smile over the scowl, the joke over the jab, flag-waving over pot-stirring, general consensus over ideological purity made for a happier country and unhappy partisans. Reagan filled his cabinet with mainstream business-oriented conservatives such as Donald Regan from Wall Street as secretary of the treasury, and old Nixon-Ford hands such as Caspar Weinberger as secretary of defense and Alexander Haig as secretary of state. The conservative grumbling that had begun during the campaign intensified. "Let Reagan be Reagan," they shouted. But in seeking the mainstream, in governing from the center, Reagan really *was* being Reagan.

At his inauguration, Reagan clarified that "it is not my intention to do away with government. It is, rather, to make it work—work with us, not over us; to stand by our side, not ride on our back." Reagan wanted to recalibrate the relationship between the government and the people, saying: "We are a nation that has a government—not the other way around."

Central to Reagan's patriotism was his optimism. He loved telling the story of two brothers. The favored brother received a beautiful blue bicycle for Christmas and grumbled that it was not red. The mistreated brother, having received a roomful of horse manure, plunged in happily, believing that so much manure must be a sign of a really big horse. "It is time for us to realize that we are too great a nation to limit ourselves to small dreams," Reagan said during his inaugural, repudiating Carter's malaise warnings. Reagan called for "an era of national renewal," challenging Americans to "renew our determination, our courage, and our strength. And let us renew our faith and our hope."

Reagan's inauguration brought the conservative movement to great power and prominence. In their wilderness years, cut off from the Harvard–Brookings–*New York Times* nexus, conservatives had developed an alternative intellectual universe. Ideologically motivated, bankrolled by frustrated corporate chieftains and entrepreneurs, an intricate network of intellectuals and strategists inhabited an overlapping world of think tanks and journals. The *National Review, Human Events, American Spectator, Commentary*, the *Public Interest*, the *National Interest*, and the essential *Wall Street Journal* circulated and recycled articles. Many writers were scholars affiliated with conservative think tanks including Stanford University's Hoover Institution, the American Enterprise Institute, Georgetown University's Center for Strategic and International Studies, and the Heritage Foundation, an aggressive newcomer focusing on Congress and the press. Marginalized by the overwhelmingly liberal university culture, these entrepreneurial ideologues improvised. The

Heritage Foundation's Academic Bank organized computerized lists of 1,600 scholars ready to mount ideological warfare at the push of a button.

Reagan's inauguration shifted the conservative movement's center of gravity to Washington, DC. No longer the symbol of evil to conservatives now that they were in charge, the capital city suddenly seemed inviting. Even as they vowed not to "go native," these young conservatives followed the paths of their New Deal and New Frontier predecessors. The Reaganauts established roots in Washington, creating a shadow government when Democrats returned to power, while pushing Republican administrations to the right.

Weeks before the inauguration, the American Enterprise Institute hosted a week-long conference. The new stars in the political firmament gleamed brightly as conservative intellectuals pitched big ideas to newly appointed officials, and wealthy businessmen wrote big checks. The highlight of the conference was the requisite—for that crowd—black-tie dinner, featuring the president-elect. "I want you to know that we'll be looking closely at your observations and proposals," Reagan cooed, telling the conservatives what they wanted to hear, promising a close "working relationship."

Over the next eight years, hundreds of "movement conservatives" would work for the Reagan administration. Many of these believers, Secretary of Education Terrel Bell recalled, "proclaimed their ideological identity on cuff links and neckties. Their logo was the profile of Adam Smith." These ideologues treated Bell contemptuously, he bristled, as someone heading "a department sired by Jimmy Carter, mothered by Congress, delivered by the National Education Association functioning as an activist midwife and publicly designated for abolition."

Like a privately held corporation, the modern presidency ostensibly reflected the boss's desires, but the hundreds of key appointees in the executive branch, managing thousands of government workers, had wide discretion. Franklin D. Roosevelt had fewer than 100 White House staffers, only 71 presidential appointees in 1933, and 50 different agencies reporting directly to him; half a century later, there were more than 350 White House staffers, 600 presidential appointees, 1,700 employees in the Executive Office of the President, and approximately two million governmental employees overall. Even without a president as open to delegating and taking direction as Reagan, the inauguration marked a sweeping changing of the guard, the debut of Ronald Reagan, Inc.

The efficiency of Reagan's White House initially rested on the leadership equivalent of a three-legged stool. Deviating from the Nixon-Ford trend toward concentrating power in one dominating chief of staff, a triumvirate led. The patrician chief of staff, James A. Baker III, a crony of Vice President George Bush, represented the Republican establishment's stability and the corporate community's financial interests. The slick deputy chief of staff, Michael Deaver, a confidante of Nancy Reagan from the world of public relations, focused on the Reagans' personal needs and the president's political image. And the professorial Edwin Meese III, who had advised Reagan as governor, was the ideologue. Baker's corporate sensibilities and Deaver's image-making calculations tempered Meese's conservatism. These three headed a Reagan team that was moderate enough to frustrate conservatives but conservative enough to terrify liberals.

The triumvirate's initial success helped feed the Reagan legend. Many critics first mocked Reagan's work ethic, as he boasted about working nine-to-five, saying, "I know that hard work never killed anyone, but I figure, why take the chance?" But his strategy of serving as a visionary CEO rather than a Jimmy Carter–like micromanager doling out playing time on the White House tennis courts, soon charmed reporters—and business executives. During the second term, when one autocratic, controversial chief of staff, Donald Regan, replaced the triumvirate, Reagan's hands-off management style would be considered more problematic.

As the Reaganites marched into Washington, issuing marching orders to the nation, Democrats remained shell-shocked. The two true-blue conservative cabinet members among the mostly moderate millionaires, David Stockman and James Watt, represented two competing impulses within conservatism. Stockman, the Office of Management and Budget director, was a technocrat with the soul of a calculator. He focussed on cutting the budget to shrink government. His methods tended to be systematic, rational, encyclopedic, delving into the complexities of the federal budget to cut, cut, cut. James Watt, on the other hand, was a fire-and-brimstone conservative with the soul of a preacher—and the subtlety of a hurricane. As a secretary of the interior hostile to environmentalism, he represented the conservatives' broader social agenda to roll back the sixties revolution and reinvigorate capitalism. Watt outraged environmentalists by selling off public lands, resisting efforts to declare species endangered, encouraging more mining, drilling, and developing, while denouncing liberals as socialists.

Reagan launched his administration with some great news—and some bad news. The great news was that during his inauguration, the Iranians finally freed their diplomatic hostages. Ayatollah Khomeini gave the most conservative, nationalistic, and aggressive American president in a generation a welcome gift. Reagan reinforced his patriotic paeans with a hostage homecoming. Many Americans decided that Reagan's more muscular rhetoric scared the mullahs, further legitimizing the conservative revolution.

Weeks later, on February 5, Reagan delivered sobering news on national television. The economy was even worse than he feared. Reagan used this news to justify even more sweeping budget cuts and tax cuts, challenging Americans to revolutionize their government.

Reagan toned down his conservatism with compassion, or at least the politically popular appearance thereof. In legitimizing "entitlements'" and maintaining the "social safety net," Reagan accepted the strong American consensus supporting the welfare state. David Stockman did not "think people are entitled to any services." Reagan, the child of Depression, acknowledged the government's responsibility to protect the "truly needy." Early in February Reagan deemed untouchable seven basic social programs serving 80 million people, costing $210 billion annually: Social Security's Old Age and Survivors Insurance; Medicare's health program for the elderly; the Veterans Administration disabilities program; Supplemental Security Income for the blind, disabled, and elderly poor; school lunch and breakfasts for low-income children; Head Start preschool services; and the Summer Youth Jobs Program. This pronouncement limited Reagan's revolution. With entitlement programs consuming approximately 60 percent of federal expenditures, and half of these programs subject to automatic Cost of Living Adjustments (COLAs), Reagan could only budget-cut on the margins.

A multifront political war began. Republicans and Democrats clashed in Congress. Liberals and conservatives dueled on the opinion pages of newspapers. And voters looked on astounded as David Stockman questioned many of the New Deal's governing assumptions and most basic programs, but then Reagan, or one of his cabinet members, backpedaled, protecting the status quo more than Reagan's reputation suggested.

Still, his rival Tip O'Neill denounced Reagan's aggressive, heartless, "Godfather tactics." The Speaker of the House alternated between grumbling about such "cold, tough and cruel" White House politicking "for the wealthy of America" and lamenting that Jimmy Carter was never so effective. O'Neill and his aides enjoyed ridiculing the president, mocking Reagan's intelligence with zingers about Reagan's reliance on note cards or coaching when lobbying Congress. Yet in the arena of congressional relations during that first year, Reagan's intelligence shone through, in the persuasive speeches he delivered, in the subtle assessments he offered his aides of legislators' positions after calling them one more time, and in the quick responses he filled out on forms staffers prepared summarizing congressional correspondence. To one congressman's "strong opposition" to Reagan's proposal for reforming Social Security, the president wrote "can he do better?" To another complaint about "a lack of leadership" in the past regarding refugee issues, the president joshed "but we don't have a lack of leadership now—or do we?"

Reagan's greatest contribution to the budget fight was in public as the "seller" he saw himself to be. Repudiating the Johnson-Nixon-Ford-Carter legacy of failure, Reagan took command immediately. He impressed large and small audiences, demonstrating the eloquence, charm, and unexpected doggedness that would shape his reputation. Skeptics were surprised that this supposed clod was quite witty; that this supposed fanatic was quite nimble—and adept—at defusing conflict. When asked about labor union opposition, he quipped, "I happen to believe that sometimes they're out of step with their own rank and file. They certainly were in the last election." When asked while chatting with reporters on Air Force One to assess a major economic address he had just delivered, the old actor admitted he was pleased, saying "but then you're always in good spirits when you figure you got by without losing your place or forgetting your lines."

Nevertheless, the salesman-in-chief failed to make the sale. The intense congressional and media backlash damaged Reagan's poll ratings by mid-March, barely two months into the administration. Polls also showed a dichotomy that would persist throughout his tenure. Reagan himself was much more popular than his programs; more Americans liked Reagan than agreed with him.

While Reagan was selling his program to union leaders at the Washington Hilton on March 30, 1981, he was shot. A disturbed twenty-six-year-old, John Hinckley, hoping to impress the actress Jodie Foster, began firing as Reagan exited the hotel. One Secret Service agent, one local police officer, and one Reagan aide, White House Press Secretary James Brady, fell to the ground, wounded. One bullet glanced off the armored limousine's door and hit Reagan. The slowed momentum of the deflected shot saved his life—but the bullet came dangerously close to his heart. Unbeknownst to most Americans, the president of the United States nearly died.

Acting with remarkable aplomb, Reagan walked stiffly from his car into the emergency room, to reassure his constituents, then collapsed. Before succumbing to the anesthetic, he delivered the first of many quips that would help build his legend. Looking at the doctor rushing him into surgery, the old actor—and partisan— asked, "I hope you're a Republican." The head surgeon, Dr. Joseph Giordano, a liberal Democrat, supposedly replied, "Mr. President, today we are all Republicans."

The failed assassination made Reagan appear larger than life and his program more politically popular than it otherwise would have been. Reagan had already emerged as a man most Americans loved to like. After the shooting, Americans rallied around their president, their country, and his policies, at least for a few months. By May 8, just over one hundred days after the inauguration, the Democratic-controlled House of Representatives passed Reagan's budget 270–154. HOUSE PASSES DEEPEST BUDGET CUT IN HISTORY, the *Los Angeles Times* proclaimed, declaring the sixty-vote margin A BIG VICTORY FOR PRESIDENT.

The Reagan revolution's first round reduced the personal income tax rate by almost one quarter, dropped the capital gains tax from 28 to 20 percent, yielding an unprecedented tax reduction of $162 billion. By the summer, Reagan had cut $35 billion in domestic spending from Jimmy Carter's request, while increasing military spending. By 1986 the defense budget would be twice 1980's allocation. "We have done more than merely trim the federal budget and reduce taxes," Reagan rejoiced. "We have boldly reversed the trend of government. As we promised to do in 1980, we have begun to trust the people to make their own decisions, by restoring their economic independence."

That summer of 1981, Ronald Reagan moved dramatically to the center on social issues. On July 7 he nominated the first woman to the Supreme Court. Sandra Day O'Connor was an Arizona Republican warmly endorsed by Senator Barry Goldwater. Many conservatives worried she was too moderate. "I am going forward on this first court appointment with a woman to get my campaign promise out of the way," Reagan told William F. Buckley, in a rare acknowledgment of brusque political calculation. Reagan added: "I'm happy to say I had to make no compromise with quality." Reagan, who prided himself on being even-tempered, bristled when local Arizona conservatives questioned O'Connor's commitment to the "pro-life" movement. In fact, O'Connor became an important swing vote who helped maintain the emerging liberal status quo on abortion and other issues dear to conservatives.

Characteristically, a few weeks later, Reagan countered by moving rightward. In early August, the Air Traffic Controllers' union, called PATCO, declared a strike. Reagan had befriended the union leaders during the campaign but had warned them during negotiations that federal government employees were banned from striking. When the controllers walked off the job, for Reagan it became a simple issue. "That's against the law," he noted in his diary. "I'm going to announce that those who strike have lost their jobs & will not be re-hired."

Reagan was taking a bold risk. At the height of the summer travel season, millions of stranded Americans could have blamed him for ruining their vacations. More sobering than the political danger was the actual danger. A major airline crash blamed on incompetent replacement workers Reagan's intransigence imposed on the system could have been disastrous.

Instead, Reagan's luck held; on this issue he demonstrated perfect political pitch. Nearly half a century after the labor gains of the 1930s, the public had lost patience with unions. Labor leaders no longer appeared to be noble warriors delivering basic rights to the great unwashed, but corrupt insiders lining their pockets at their members'—and the public's—expense. Reagan rode this backlash. On August 4, the day after Reagan read the "written oath each employee signs" not to strike, a third of the controllers had returned to work. Flying was 65 percent normal. The next day nearly 40 percent worked, with air traffic at 75 percent normal.

Reagan's strong stand against the air traffic controllers devastated the already weakened labor movement but provoked widespread applause. In many ways, this move defined his first year in office. Reagan showed there was a new sheriff in town. Millions of Americans welcomed such affirmative leadership after decades of drift. Corporate leaders on both sides of the Atlantic also applauded the pro-business stance. Years later, when explaining how America tamed inflation and emerged from the economic doldrums, the chairman of the Federal Reserve Board at the time, Paul Volcker, would call the PATCO showdown a turning point in America's economic, psychic, and patriotic revival.

On August 13, shortly after his PATCO star-turn, Reagan signed his tax-cutting legislation at his California ranch. The president of the United States wore a denim suit with an open-necked collar.

Photographers captured him turning in his seat at an outdoor table with stacks of bills to sign and a microphone, kicking up a booted foot and beaming.

Ronald Reagan had a lot to smile about. This was the Reagan Revolution's happy face. In eight months, he had silenced many of the doubts surrounding him while freeing Americans of some of the self-doubt that had been clinging to them. Americans were feeling prouder, more nationalistic, more in control, thrilled to have a president who was proud, assertive, and affirmative. Reagan's assault on the ways of the New Deal and the Great Society was progressing. His tax cuts and his strike-breaking were popular. Ronald Reagan could claim he led Americans on a great rediscovery of their values—and of their common sense.

But close observers could also see the limits to Reagan's don't-rock-the-boat revolution. He had tweaked the governing New Deal status quo without really assailing it. Much of the budget fight

5. Ronald Reagan at his ranch after signing historic tax-cutting legislation on August 13, 1981.

remained about the margins of growth rather than the fundamental assumptions of what Reagan always called "big guvment." And, as with the Sandra Day O'Connor appointment and other critical moves, Reagan recognized the needs to mollify the media, the Democrats, and the majority of American people who doubted his program, even if they liked him.

The dramatic changes Prime Minister Margaret Thatcher implemented in Great Britain demonstrated President Reagan's constraints—and more limited accomplishments. Thatcher became prime minister in 1979, eighteen months before Reagan's inauguration. Like Reagan, she sought to cut the budget, reduce taxes, and diminish union power. But Great Britain's welfare state was much more elaborate and entrenched. Nevertheless, Mrs. Thatcher had more latitude, given the prime minister's control of the Parliament and Parliament's primacy in the British system. Thatcher reduced the basic tax rate from 33 percent to 25 percent, dropping the top rate from as high as 98 percent—83 percent on wages and a 15 percent surcharge on interest and dividends—to 40 percent. She opened capital markets, confronted many more unions than Reagan did, and privatized some major British industries including British Airways and British Steel.

Still, while Thatcher's record may eclipse Reagan's, her calls for revolution reinforced his. That both Great Britain and the United States had vigorous, conservative leaders calling for small government and freer enterprise generated an impression that liberalism was retreating and that the conservative revolution was global. Thatcher visited Reagan on February 26, 1981, a little more than a month into Reagan's tenure. Reagan greeted her warmly, saying "We believe that our solutions lie within the people and not the state." Thatcher replied: "Mr. President, the natural bond of interest between our two countries is strengthened by the common approach which you and I have to our national problems.... We are both trying to set free the energies of our

6. President Reagan greeting British prime minister Margaret Thatcher at the White House, February 26, 1981.

people. We are both determined to sweep away the restrictions that hold back enterprise."

Reagan was already mastering his governing formula. He understood that in the modern American politics of spin, the illusion of action was often as important as the action itself. Reagan was happy to talk right and govern center, to champion conservatism but act moderately, to hear others talk about a "Reagan Revolution," but keep the discussion more limited to his Great Rediscovery.

Thus, the revolution did not follow Reagan's stated script. The ship of state did not veer sharply to the right. However, Reagan helped reorient America, changing the country's approach to questions of budget, big government, and the welfare state. A new vocabulary of budget cutting, tax cutting, and deregulation took hold. In the long term, these shifts changed America's trajectory. Simultaneously, the resulting great prosperity of the 1980s fed a more individualistic approach and intensified many of the trends toward a more consumer-driven, celebrity-oriented, and selfish society—which Reagan came to personify in many ways, even as he tempered it with a veneer of traditionalist rhetoric.

Chapter 5

Did the Democrats fiddle as the Reaganauts conquered Washington?

In 1981, headlines blared about Democratic disarray as Republicans celebrated their self-fulfilling claim of a Reagan mandate. Democrats were divided, unsure whether to fight Reaganism relentlessly or allow this new experiment to progress—and fail. "I do not and will not accept the widely held view that Governor Reagan is entitled to a 'honeymoon' and that our Party should stand quietly aside," the incoming Democratic National Committee chairman Charles Manatt wrote to the Democratic Speaker of the House Tip O'Neill in January 1981. "We must stand by our Democratic principles and I will be a strong spokesperson for that view."

Despite the bravado, most Democrats, including Manatt initially, dodged confrontation. Yet claims that the Reaganauts dominated Washington and undid the New Deal are overstated. By autumn 1981 the Democrats had started checking the Reagan Revolution with the "Fairness Issue," charging that the Republican tax cuts and budget cuts favored the rich at the poor's expense. Democrats would claw back from the 1980 losses, holding their majority in the House of Representatives and recapturing the Senate in 1986. Congressional relations would become so strained that when a farmers' group offered President Reagan a gift of a mule, he refused saying: "I'm afraid I can't use a mule. I have several hundred up on Capitol Hill." Meanwhile, the Democratic-driven revolutions in so many areas of American life, including civil rights, sex, environmentalism, and consumerism, continued—and intensified.

Instead of Charles Manatt, the Democrat who most effectively confronted Ronald Reagan was Tip O'Neill. O'Neill was easily caricatured with his mane of white hair, bulbous nose, beefy appearance, working-class Massachusetts accent, and quick, rumbly, laugh. Although a creature of the congressional backrooms, once he realized he had become the Democrats' national spokesman, O'Neill adapted to the television era. He lost forty pounds. He bought new suits. He accepted media training. And he began speaking in sound bites, defending the welfare state.

A clever tactician, O'Neill preserved many Great Society programs by defending the New Deal. He understood that

7. President Reagan hosts Speaker of the House Tip O'Neill at the White House in January 1986, with Vice President George H. W. Bush looking on.

Reagan played to Americans' frustrations with the dashed hopes from the War on Poverty and the Civil Rights movement. But O'Neill also understood that generations of Americans had already grown up taking for granted the basic security Franklin Roosevelt delivered—and that Reagan himself still worshiped Roosevelt.

Even so, it took months for O'Neill to find his footing. During the Reagan administration's heady first few months, many Americans fearing another presidential failure demanded that the Speaker give Reagan a chance. In Congress, O'Neill faced a steamroller of a united Republican caucus bolstered by conservative southern "Boll Weevil" Democrats.

O'Neill tried maintaining Democrats' morale during the first round of Reagan victories. By September 1981, O'Neill was ready. Reporters happily publicized his portrait of Reagan the reverse Robin Hood, stealing from the poor to serve the rich. Stories of people unfairly thrown off food stamps, of kids suffering in schools, of growing lineups to get dwindling services made great television. O'Neill also exploited Reagan's success. When Congress members returned from the summer recess, retelling constituents' tales of economic woe, O'Neill could blame the new president, not Jimmy Carter, for "The Reagan Recession."

Reagan and his aides particularly resented the charges of unfairness and economic elitism. The New Deal–Great Society status quo still prevailed. Torn between his desire for sympathetic headlines and his disdain for big government, Reagan boasted that "We are providing 95 million meals a day—that is 1/7th of all the meals in this country; providing medical care for 47 million Americans and subsidized housing for more than 10 million." Reagan's Legislative Strategy Group debated: "how do we sustain: bipartisan spirit (or quest therefore); positive association with interest in fairness; [and] movement toward a practical program of deficit reduction/economic recovery?"

The recession ruined Reagan's second year in office and derailed the Reagan juggernaut. Paul Volcker, the Federal Reserve chairman, stopped the galloping inflation of the Carter years. Reagan did not interfere as Volcker set interest rates and agreed to raise taxes when pressed. This strategy worked economically in the long run but was politically disastrous. Unemployment hit a post–Great Depression high of 10.8 percent, affecting 12 million workers; Reagan's legislative program languished as attacks on Reaganism and Reagan intensified. From the sidelines, former president Richard Nixon advised that Reagan needed an aggressive partisan to counterattack, just as he had done for Dwight Eisenhower, and Spiro Agnew had done for him. Reagan's sophomore slump was so bad that pundits began eulogizing his presidency, bemoaning yet another presidential failure.

Reagan's honey-smooth refusal to take responsibility for the recession frustrated Democrats and pundits. As one press conference ended, ABC's pugnacious reporter Sam Donaldson barked: "Mr. President, in talking about the continuing recession tonight, you have blamed the mistakes of the past and you've blamed the Congress. Does any of the blame belong to you?" Reagan quickly replied, "Yes, because for many years I was a Democrat." Such exchanges fed the caricature of Reagan as heartless and clueless. But these witty improvisations also reflected the light touch and political agility that made him popular and elevated his post-presidential reputation.

In 1982 Reagan acted responsibly by agreeing to "revenue enhancements"—what taxpayers and IRS agents called tax hikes. The $37.5 billion Tax Equity and Fiscal Responsibility Act of 1982 limited the galloping deficits. The Highway Revenue Act added another $3.3 billion to government coffers via a gasoline tax increase. Reagan appealed to legislators' "spirit of bipartisanship and compromise." That July, forty-two conservatives charged the tax hike "undermines" Reagan's "original economic recovery plan and reneges on his pledge not to balance the budget on the backs of the American taxpayer." Ten congressmen, including Newt Gingrich and Jack Kemp, denounced "the largest peacetime legislated tax increase in history." Still, a year later Reagan signed an increase in the Social Security tax rate and in 1984, he signed the Deficit Reduction Act raising taxes by $18 billion annually.

The 1982 midterm elections further sobered Republicans and energized Democrats. The Democrats triumphed with their hard-hitting slogan: "It's not fair: it's Republican." O'Neill felt vindicated. The twenty-seven new Democratic House seats restored the losses from 1980, although the Senate remained Republican with the Democrats picking up only one seat, formerly held by a Democratic-leaning independent.

Despite Republicans' midterm election loss, the recession was well timed. It came early enough in Reagan's term for the economy, and his reputation, to recover. And the bitter medicine Dr. Volcker prescribed, with Dr. Reagan's passive acceptance, did its magic. Interest rates and the inflation rate dropped as the recession lingered. Then, starting in late 1982, an impressive economic boom began. The Federal Reserve's monetary policy and the new Reagan-induced business confidence fueled this surge, but so did deeper structural forces.

Much of the 1980s' success was rooted in the 1970s. Reeling from the oil crisis, America's traditionally static car manufacturers began adapting. Other corporate dinosaurs learned to replace the 1950s' rigid hierarchies with more nimble structures. The baby boomers also flourished as earners and innovators, no longer students and agitators. The result was an eruption of new inventions, new ways of doing business, new businesses. Households became revolutionized. VCRs and PCs filled dens, microwaves and food processers crowded kitchen counters. Silicon Valley and the computer revolution took off, as did the financial revolution on Wall Street.

Characteristically, the Reagan PR machine boosted the recovery before it even began. As the recession persisted in autumn 1982, the administration celebrated the 25 percent drop in tax rates and inflation's plunge "from 12.4% in 1980 to 4.8% in 1982." Both shifts injected more dollars into Americans' pockets. White House strategy memos noted that "the President's approval rating is strongly influenced by inflation," while "Unemployment has little impact on presidential popularity."

By 1983 Reaganite optimism blossomed into euphoria as the economy created more than 1.1 million new jobs. The Dow Jones average set a record, passing the 1100 mark. Housing starts rose to their highest level since December 1978. The annual inflation rate dropped to the lowest level since October 1967. That October, when this benchmark-obsessed administration celebrated one thousand days in office, Reagan toasted America's improved "quality of life," thanks to "an industrial renaissance," fueled by venture capital and "products of high technology." Reagan declared: "Our quality of life is improving because your voices, voices of common sense, are finally getting through. Believe me, it wasn't Washington experts who said government is too big, taxes are too high, criminals are coddled, education's basics are neglected and values of family and faith are being undermined. That was your message. You made reforms possible." Here was the Reagan narrative with a twist— rather than taking the credit himself, the president reflected it back to the country.

Ronald Reagan floated to re-election in 1984 on the waves of optimism this boom unleashed. His "Morning in America" campaign suited America's mood. Just as the 1984 Olympics in Los Angeles became a mass celebration of America's renewal, Reagan's campaign celebrated America's patriotic resurgence. Most Americans happily buried the 1960s' divisions and headaches, the 1970s' warnings and messes.

The Democrats found 1984 particularly confusing. Mired in the critiques of the sixties and the despair of the seventies, outraged by the excesses of the eighties, partisans and journalists mocked all this rah-rah-sis-boom-bah patriotism. The Democratic nominee, Jimmy Carter's vice president, Walter Mondale, watched his poll ratings drop from the fall of 1983, when surveys predicted he would beat Reagan handily.

Mondale's "Norwegian charisma," as one wag joked, made him a particularly hapless Reagan rival. Two fiery orators upstaged Mondale at his own Democratic Convention. New York's Governor Mario Cuomo thundered that Reagan's beloved metaphor delighting in America as a "shining city on a hill" was a mirage: "this Nation is more a 'Tale of Two Cities,'" one thriving, the other languishing. But Cuomo's bracing message seemed shrill compared to Reagan's good vibrations. And Cuomo's "Democratic credo"—"We believe in only the government we need, but we insist on all the government we need"—revealed a new, Reaganesque ambivalence about government. Similarly, the African American activist, the Reverend Jesse Jackson, delivered a multicultural message too divisive to compete with Reagan's unifying nationalism. "Our flag is red, white and blue, but our Nation is a rainbow," Jackson preached, "Red, Yellow, Brown, Black and White—we're all precious in God's sight."

Mondale excited Democrats by nominating Geraldine Ferraro, a Queens congresswoman, as the first woman on a major party national ticket. But Ferraro mostly energized Mondale's base and proved too controversial. Fellow Catholics denounced her pro-choice stand, making her one of many Democratic casualties from the Reagan-era culture wars. Reporters also hounded Ferraro about her husband's dishonest accounting practices, which included siphoning $175,000 from an elderly widow's estate. Such "gotcha" scandal-mongering would derail both Republicans and Democrats, undermining Americans' faith in politics at a time when political corruption actually was declining.

Walter Mondale—or "Walter Mondull" as one disappointed Democrat sighed—lacked even Cuomo's programmatic passion or Jackson's lyrical radicalism. Like so many reporters, Mondale trusted the printed word and the power of facts to refute Reagan's warm fuzzy image-making. Republicans pooh-poohed the Democrats' statistical barrage along with the nitpicking, claiming, as White House communications director David Gergen once did, that "making sure we have every single fact straight" is less important than "whether the larger points are right."

The Reagan-Mondale showdown did not just pit Reaganite Republicanism against Democratic liberalism. The emerging Republican Sun Belt confronted the decaying Democratic Rust Belt. It was the old politics versus the new, the old culture versus the new, a campaign of images, ads, and well-choreographed balloon drops versus a campaign of ideas, speeches, and well-intentioned but often sparsely attended union rallies.

Reagan won forty-nine states and more electoral votes, 525, than any previous victor. Mondale's tally of thirteen electoral votes was the lowest Democratic total ever. Yet this victory came at a cost. Ronald Reagan's apple-pie, feel-good campaign secured a second presidential term with minimal congressional backing. Republicans gained sixteen seats in the House of Representatives, remaining the minority, and lost two Senate seats.

The sounds of the brass bands may have drowned out the chorus of critics, but the criticisms remained. Reagan's campaign further alienated those who felt excluded from his nationwide party. And the mushy mandate for peace and prosperity—without a congressional majority—haunted his second term. During his second four years in office, Reagan would never match the intensity, or forge the same apparent national consensus, he mobilized in 1981.

The seeming excesses of the Yuppie and the broader "money culture" only confirmed Democrats' critique of Reaganism as economic elitism. Many intellectuals argued that compared to the 1980s, both the 1950s and the 1920s were benign, or even progressive. During the Reagan era, the long-standing "marriage of economic wealth and political power has been solemnized anew," the *New Republic* mourned. "Under the Reagan dispensation, shame is banished, greed enshrined, and the political supremacy of private wealth celebrated as frankly as it was in the Gilded Age."

This sustained counterattack impeded Reaganism without repudiating it. As a result, two contradictory conceptions governed 1980s politics. Most Americans still accepted Reagan's diagnosis of America's ailments and questioned the government's ability to solve problems. But most Americans joined the Democrats in doubting Reagan's cure, further undermining their faith in government and their leaders.

By 1986 the Democrats were on the march, facing a tired, defensive administration, lacking the snap of the first-term team. In the midterm elections, Democrats in the House gained only five seats, but Democrats in the Senate gained eight, unseating many of the freshman incumbents first elected on Ronald Reagan's coattails in 1981. The Democrats recaptured control of the Senate, securing a comfortable 55–45 majority. With Democrats back controlling both Houses, Reagan's legislative agenda became even more limited.

The implications of the loss of the Senate became clear a year later, when Ronald Reagan endured a particularly traumatic month. In November 1987, his mother-in-law died, his wife underwent breast-cancer surgery, the stock market crashed, and the Senate rejected his Supreme Court nominee, Robert Bork. Bork's rejection highlighted the limits of Reagan's power and marked the end of any aspirations to revolution.

The Bork confirmation debacle obscured Reagan's broader success in transforming the federal judiciary. Reagan and his Justice Department aides systematically recruited young, healthy, conservative ideologues to serve on the federal bench. Most reporters concentrated on the Supreme Court setback, forgetting that Reagan appointed three of the nine judges and promoted William Rehnquist, an Arizona conservative, to chief justice. Overall, Reagan's seventy-eight new appellate court judges—out of a total of 167 appellate court judgeships—collectively helped reorient American law. The appointees were too tied to judicial precedent and the status quo to undo the Warren Court revolution of the 1950s and the 1960s. Still, the federal judiciary deferred more to state and presidential prerogatives, tried limiting but not outlawing abortion, and more regularly resisted attempts to extend federal power.

Reagan's executive appointments also penetrated through many levels of Washington's vast bureaucracies. A new generation of government employees skeptical about government's effectiveness transformed Washington. They often worked side by side—and clashed—with liberal peers who believed in the bureaucracies they served. By 1986 Reaganites had halved the Federal Register, the bible of federal regulations. Reaganism could not stop the welfare state's momentum as government grew, but he lowered the rate of that growth, and his government abandoned some of his predecessors' initiatives in areas including civil rights and safety.

Regarding social issues, as so many of 1960s' lifestyle and attitude revolutions became mainstreamed, there was a Reagan Reconciliation more than a rollback. All but the most radical conservatives accepted certain irrevocable advances, especially regarding black and female equality. In not ending certain initiatives, in embracing many causes often considered to be liberal, and in reaching out to both blacks and women, Reagan helped institutionalize and legitimize the changes—just as Dwight Eisenhower had done with New Deal reforms. But the movements championing these changes often felt embattled, even as their ideas became normalized. Like most Democrats, the advocates for civil rights, feminism, gay liberation, and environmentalism felt thwarted despite their tremendous progress.

As Americans cheered Reagan's odes to old-fashioned, small-town, and implicitly monochromatic America, a new, urbanized, and dizzyingly diverse country emerged. Two decades after the 1964 Civil Rights Act passed, even though black–white relations seemed mired in fights over affirmative action, busing, and crime, the civil rights revolution continued. Racism was no longer acceptable in public or in polite company. Polls showed that 98 percent of whites did not object to blacks moving in next door, 95 percent accepted bosses who were black, 89 percent would go to a black doctor, and 85 percent approved of their children hosting black playmates. Even if whites exaggerated their openness, these dramatic attitude shifts created a new, more open-minded, more civil civic culture.

African Americans streamed into America's middle class, joining important institutions essential to their eventual success. The number of black undergraduates grew exponentially, from 125,000 in 1950 to more than 2 million in 1988. Four hundred thousand blacks served in perhaps America's most color-blind institution, the military, constituting 20 percent of the overall force. Blacks were moving into previously segregated neighborhoods, enrolling in formerly lily-white elite schools, and making their marks not only as doctors, lawyers, and corporate executives in previously closed professions but also as police officers, fire fighters, electricians, and members of previously closed unions.

African Americans became healthier too. Their life expectancy increased by 5.6 years to 69.7 from 1970 to 1987. The still-too-high infant mortality rate dropped from 32.6 deaths per thousand in 1970 to 18 per thousand in 1986.

The success of second- and third-generation European immigrants, Italians, Greeks, and Jews, once dismissed as "swarthy" and "primitive" "foreigners," encouraged the real stars of 1980s immigration, the Hispanics and Asians. Two decades after Lyndon Johnson's 1965 immigration reforms cancelled the 1920s' Eurocentric national origins legislation, streams of immigrants from Asia, Africa, and Latin America changed the face of America. When Jesse Jackson talked about a rainbow coalition, most Americans thought about blacks and whites. America truly was becoming a multicultural, multiethnic polyglot. From 1950 to 1990 the United States would absorb nearly 20 million legal immigrants, 8.3 million in the 1980s alone, accounting for one-third of America's population growth. By 1990 foreign-born residents constituted 8 percent of the census. The Hispanic presence increased by more than 60 percent in the 1970s and another 50 percent in the 1980s. By 1995 there would be 27 million Hispanics. Pessimists, such as the conservative Pat Buchanan, warned that the flood of illegal immigrants further demonstrated governmental impotence and imported social turmoil. Optimists, such as the demographer Ben Wattenberg, delighted in this renewed immigration as a welcome engine of economic growth and a reminder of America's ideological destiny.

Similarly, even as many young women benefiting from feminism rejected the "F-word," and the Equal Rights Amendment institutionalizing gender equality in the Constitution failed to win ratification by enough states, gender equity became institutionalized. The supposed archconservative Ronald Reagan nominated the first female Supreme Court justice and presided over a cabinet that consistently had two or three women at the table. By 1980 the number of working women doubled from 19.5 million in 1955 to more than 42 million. More than half the women in the United States were employed or seeking work outside the home; only a third were solely homemakers. The working women were younger, the homemakers older. In 1980, for the first time the Census Bureau stopped defining husbands as the only possible "heads of households," with four of ten marriages ending in divorce.

As women exercised more political power as a group, Republicans struggled with the growing "gender gap." Single women, in particular, were increasingly hostile to the Republican Party. White House aides worked hard to mollify women. Like his predecessors, Ronald Reagan ritualistically listed all the women he had appointed to high positions, met with his female appointees regularly, appointed women to recruit more women, and boasted about how his administration had been better to women than any other. Aides recognized that Reagan's opposition to legalized abortion and the ratification of the Equal Rights Amendment alienated feminists. One critic blasted his "outdated" and insulting "Me-Tarzan-You-Jane Approach to male-female relations." Still, Reagan and his staff understood that reaching out to blacks and women was important to moderate the president's image, even if it rarely mollified the activists.

The administration also advanced environmentalism more than Reagan or his critics ever expected. When Reagan was elected, NBC News pronounced "the end of the environmental movement," along with the demise of feminism and civil rights. Reagan and many conservatives loved the outdoors. They embraced Theodore Roosevelt's conservation tradition. But they feared the environmental movement as anticapitalist, big government-oriented, and too hostile to what they and their corporate supporters defined as progress. In appointing the conservative ideologue James Watt as interior secretary and the inexperienced Anne Gorsuch to head the Environmental Protection Agency, Reagan seemingly confirmed the most pessimistic of predictions.

Nevertheless, since the early 1960s when the writer Rachel Carson spelled out just how bleak a "Silent Spring" pollution could create, Americans had increasingly tolerated federal intervention to clean the atmosphere. The Reaganites recognized that, as with civil rights, they could not assail environmentalism directly. Instead, they would use the economic crisis to try justifying rollbacks. "The Reagan Administration's environmental policy is premised on the fact that only a strong economy can support a clean and improving environment. Hungry people, people without homes and jobs to support their families cannot afford to be environmentalists," the Reagan White Paper on Environmental Policy proclaimed. This would not be a crusade, but a balancing act.

"Preservation of our environment is not a liberal or conservative challenge—it's common sense," Reagan declared in the 1984 State of the Union speech. By 1985 Reagan had added 2.5 million acres to federally protected lands and boosted EPA's proposed 1985 budget by 53 percent over 1983. That would be "the largest nondefense-spending increase in the budget" and include "a tripling of toxic-dump-cleanup funds," according to *U.S. News and World Report*. Prodded by grassroots campaigns, the Sierra Club's magazine, *Sierra*, reported, "more acreage was added to the National Wilderness Preservation System in the lower 48 states under Reagan than under any other president. Twenty-nine new wildlife refuges were established, encompassing a total of 500,000 acres; 200 new plants and animals were added to the nation's lists of endangered species. The Clean Water Act, the Resources Conservation and Recovery Act, and the Comprehensive Environmental Response, Compensation, and Liability Act (the Superfund) have all been reauthorized and greatly strengthened."

While Reagan modified his course, the environmental movement grew, partially out of alarm regarding Reagan's intentions. Membership in the Sierra Club jumped from 181,000 to 365,000 by 1983, and to more than 480,000 by 1988. By 1988 the *Sierra* reported that Reagan's anti-environmental reputation "strengthened, rather than weakened, the public's determination to protect the environment, and that is one of the more surprising legacies of Ronald Reagan."

To a surprising extent, Democrats and liberals held their own during the Reagan Revolution. Both Democrats and Republicans tended to exaggerate Republican gains and Democratic losses. But the Democrats demonstrated more political strength than they anticipated, and their core ideals persevered more than Republicans wanted to admit. Reagan's attempt at revolution showed that many seemingly radical innovations from the 1960s had become fundamental policies and core ideals. Despite Reagan's conservative rhetoric and popularity, twentieth-century America remained shaped by Franklin Roosevelt's liberalism and the 1960s counterculture. The anti-Reagan resistance was so effective there would be no real need for a counterrevolution; even as the Reagan rediscovery would be so effective, there would be no cry for a counterrevolution. The result was a country more conservative than it was before Reagan was elected, but more divided and more ambivalent than simplistic headlines usually suggested.

Chapter 6

Who ended the Cold War—
Reagan or Gorbachev?

When Ronald Reagan became president, the *Bulletin of Atomic Scientists* moved the hands of its famous doomsday clock closer to midnight. This ominous shift on the cover of a sober, academic journal reflected the intellectual and liberal hysteria that greeted Reagan's inauguration. Predictions abounded of unnecessary conflicts with the Soviet Union, of violations of the Cold War's painstakingly improvised protocols, and of nuclear war itself. And yet, two months later, while recovering from John Hinckley's bullet, Reagan wrote a surprisingly warm letter to the Soviet premier, Leonid Brezhnev. Using friendly language that the State Department tried rewriting, Reagan sought a human connection with the leader of world Communism, despite decades of demonizing Communist ideology. Reagan believed the Lord spared his life to bring peace to the world. Even more surprising was Reagan's emergence during the second term as an enthusiastic summiteer, meeting the new young Soviet premier Mikhail Gorbachev in Geneva, Reykjavik, Washington, DC, and Moscow itself.

The Soviet Union's fall shortly after Ronald Reagan's retirement triggered vigorous debates about Reagan's role in winning the Cold War. When *Time* magazine designated Gorbachev "Man of the Decade" in 1990 for peacefully neutralizing Soviet

Communism, the cover story compared Gorbachev to Freud, Copernicus, Darwin, Magellan, Martin Luther, and the Pope. Ronald Reagan was not mentioned. Two decades later, the American president and the Soviet premier are more frequently linked to explain the Cold War's happy ending. Still, questions remain regarding Reagan's centrality to this process—and how his dueling personae as the affable accommodator and the saber-rattling anti-Communist shaped this momentous shift.

In the 1950s, even as Reagan built his worldview on anti-Communism, his pacifist Church of Christ upbringing still shaped him. Nelle Reagan raised her son to abhor war. In the 1970s, his revulsion for Communism mingled with his disdain for bureaucrats who banked on the mutual threat of massive nuclear annihilation to restrain both the Americans and the Soviets. Reagan rejected this doctrine of Mutual Assured Destruction (MAD) as mad itself.

At the same time, Reagan doubted the Nixon-era détente policy and distrusted the Soviet Communists. Defiance of Soviet policy lay at the heart of Reagan's defense buildup, his Central American policy, even, to an extent, his renewal of American morale. Early in his tenure, mocking claims that his foreign policy was simplistic, the president summarized his message for the Soviets: "Roses are red, violets are blue. Stay out of El Salvador, and Poland too."

Reagan's nationalist revivalism infused his foreign policy. In celebrating America as John Winthrop's "city upon a hill with the eyes of all people upon us," as Alexis de Tocqueville's "land of wonders," Reagan asserted his anti-Communism. Central to the Reagan narrative was the claim that he restored American standing throughout the world, after the humiliations of the Jimmy Carter years—and earlier. Reagan proudly quoted U.N. Ambassador Jeane Kirkpatrick's assessment that "We've taken off our 'Kick Me' sign." Supporters loved his muscular rhetoric and his refusal to apologize for the Vietnam War or other American actions.

Reagan believed in peace through strength, that a long-term accommodation with the Soviet Union could only come after some short-term intimidation. What struck liberals as contradictory was Reagan's guiding foreign policy assumption: "Our strength is necessary to deter war and to facilitate negotiated solutions.... Strength and dialog go hand in hand." Reagan eschewed hard choices. In foreign policy as in domestic policy he believed America could build up the military and count down toward peace, just as he believed America could boost defense while cutting taxes without suffering economically.

In that spirit, Reagan wanted a visionary, aggressive, resourceful, and unapologetic foreign policy. Beyond exorcising the trauma of Vietnam, he wanted to repudiate decades of what he labeled Democratic appeasement. Along with England's Margaret Thatcher and Pope John Paul II, Reagan injected a note of moral clarity into the debate. Communism's evil demanded vigilance. In preparing one defense-related speech, the president scribbled: "what must be recognized is that our security is based on being prepared to meet any contingency." That entailed a conventional and nuclear arms buildup—to achieve peace.

In confronting the Soviets, Reagan acted on the central obsession that propelled his political career. The fight against Communists, their supporters known as fellow-travelers, and cowardly liberals mobilized him in the Hollywood of the 1940s, infused his General Electric speeches in the 1950s, and propelled him toward politics in the 1960s. By the 1970s Reagan insisted that "The ideological struggle dividing the world is between communism and our own belief in freedom to the greatest extent possible consistent with an orderly society." In his radio talks and stump speeches, he defined Communism as "neither an ec[onomic] or a pol[itical] system" but "as a form of insanity—a temporary aberration which will one day disappear from the earth because it is contrary to human nature."

Reagan's anti-Communism oriented him. In a telling moment during one of the administration's worst crises, former Senator and actor George Murphy, a comrade in the fight against Communists in Hollywood, compared the critics shrieking about the Iran-Contra scandal to the liberals and fellow travelers who attacked Reagan for fighting Communism. Reagan replied warmly, agreeing that "In our Hollywood adventure with infiltration and subversion you and I picked up a lot of knowledge the pundits and the politicos don't have." No matter what the particular battle, the two old friends were still fighting the same fight.

The Vietnam debacle shattered the broad national Cold War consensus about the need to contain Communism. As America became bogged down in Indochina, as liberals and Democrats soured on an anti-Communist intervention, many seemed to forget anti-Communism's centrality to postwar liberalism. With each passing year, more and more Americans believed that had he lived, the great liberal martyr John F. Kennedy would have withdrawn from Vietnam—even though immediately after his assassination, when the Vietnam War remained popular, most insiders insisted Kennedy wanted to hang tough.

President Jimmy Carter tried repenting for Vietnam and restoring America's foreign policy luster by championing human rights. Yet the Carter administration kept stumbling overseas, with two of the biggest blows being the fall of Nicaragua and Iran to anti-American leaders. Meanwhile, Carter seemed to tolerate Soviet expansionism in Africa, Central America, and the Middle East.

Conservative intellectuals rejected the new trend of apologetic Westerners kowtowing to the Third World. Spicing their moralism with realpolitik, many distinguished between totalitarian Communists and pro-capitalist, pro-American moderate authoritarians such as the shah of Iran. Looking back, analysts such as Nixon's secretary of defense James Schlesinger would realize ideological considerations led many to overstate American weakness and Soviet military strength. Such widespread insecurity made many Americans doubt disarmament initiatives such as the SALT II Treaty. As a result, Schlesinger and others concluded, "only a president who enjoys a reputation for being strong on defense can be successful in obtaining Senate ratification of an arms control agreement with the Soviet Union."

In his 1980 presidential campaign—and throughout his administration—Reagan would work with renegade anti-Communist Democrats. Reagan's UN ambassador, Jeane Kirkpatrick, may have been the highest ranking of these neoconservatives, who populated the Defense Department, the State Department, and many pro-Reagan think tanks. These neoconservatives supported Reagan's hard line, articulated in his "Reagan Doctrine," which the conservative Heritage Foundation championed. Toughening the postwar policy of "containing" Communism, Reagan sought to roll back Communism in Angola, Cambodia, Ethiopia, Laos, Libya, Nicaragua, and Vietnam—the arenas where Soviets expanded in the 1970s. Heritage also listed Iran, although the problem there was Islamic fundamentalism, not Communism.

Paralleling Carter, Reagan's foreign policy was often personal and moralistic—but the Republican version was more muscular, nationalist, and proactive. As much as he hated nuclear weapons, Reagan felt compelled to place more missiles in Europe. Since 1977 the Soviets had started deploying their powerful SS-20 Saber, a first-strike weapon with three targetable warheads. By 1987, 654 Intermediate-range Nuclear Force (INF) missiles with 509 launchers would be aimed at Europe's major cities. Reagan wanted to respond by deploying 108 Pershing II tactical missiles and 464 land-based Tomahawk cruise missiles in Europe. In November 1983, the Soviets walked out of arms control talks with the Americans, after the West German Bundestag approved the deployment. Reagan continued seeking opportunities to negotiate while positioning the missiles.

Many European leftists blasted Reagan. Unruffled, Reagan noted the irony. During the 1970s, many Europeans, especially German chancellor Helmut Schmidt, feared Jimmy Carter's America was too pliant. They chided Carter for cancelling the neutron bomb, which killed people but kept property intact. Now that there was a tougher American president, Europeans feared he was too militant.

Ronald Reagan's foreign policy also made many Americans nervous. The Nuclear Freeze Movement thrived by mimicking his tactics, subordinating complicated policy questions to one terrifying image, in this case a mushroom cloud looming over America's heartland. In June 1982, 700,000 people flooded Central Park shouting "No Nukes." *The Day After*, ABC's November 1983 movie dramatizing the effects of a nuclear attack on Lawrence, Kansas, frightened the nation. With an estimated 100 million viewers, it would be the 1980s' ninth most-watched television show, only bested by the final episode of the long-running TV comedy series M*A*S*H and various Super Bowls. In co-sponsoring a bipartisan freeze resolution, Senator Edward Kennedy mocked Reagan's "voodoo arms control, which says you must have more in order to have less." In 1982 seventeen Senators and 128 House members supported the freeze; the next year, the House of Representatives passed a resolution calling for a freeze.

While critics of Reagan's domestic policy often resurrected the traumas of the Great Depression, critics of Reagan's foreign policy alternated between feeding the fear of Armageddon and resurrecting the ghost of Vietnam. By May 1981, thousands had massed in the capital for what reporters claimed was the "largest march" at the Pentagon since the Vietnam War. Many feared another Vietnam-like quagmire in Central America. "No draft, no war, U.S. out of El Salvador," the protesters chanted, infuriated by Reagan's aggressive anti-Communism and seeming blindness to non-Communist dictators' moral failings.

Midway through Reagan's presidency, Nixon's secretary of defense James Schlesinger would reject the extreme reactions in both Europe and the United States. "In the late 1960s and early 1970s, the national mood was one of self-criticism bordering on masochism," Schlesinger observed. "In the 1980s the national mood has become one of self-congratulation to the point of narcissism." Schlesinger preferred a less emotional, more realistic and stable stance.

Reagan considered his foreign policy "simple" and "neat." He wanted to inject moral clarity into the national quest for self-defense. During a March 8, 1983, speech at the National Association of Evangelicals' conference in Orlando, Florida, Reagan denounced the trends toward self-abasement and moral relativism. He warned the religious broadcasters to beware "the temptation of blithely declaring yourselves above it all and label both sides equally at fault, to ignore the facts of history and the aggressive impulses of an evil empire, to simply call the arms race a giant misunderstanding and thereby remove yourself from the struggle between right and wrong and good and evil." Two weeks later, Reagan sought to transcend the MAD strategy by proposing "defensive technologies," which "could intercept and destroy strategic ballistic missiles before they reached our own soil or that of our allies." Wags branded Reagan's speech calling the Soviet Union an "evil empire," the "Darth Vader" speech. Reagan's technological solution to the problem, saddled with the bureaucratic moniker of the Strategic Defense Initiative, or SDI, became known as the "Star Wars" defense.

Reagan's calling the Soviet Union an "evil empire" was a defining moment. Furious liberals called him "primitive," "embarrassing," and unduly aggressive. But Reagan's "Rambo" rhetoric seized most Americans' imaginations. His muscular foreign policy resonated in Hollywood, where Sylvester Stallone and Arnold Schwarzenegger played beefed-up and often renegade sheriffs ensuring justice the world over—thus helping Americans overcome feelings of impotence from the crime wave back home. The "evil empire" language also allied America's president with two other iconoclastic visionaries of the 1980s, British prime minister Margaret Thatcher and Pope John Paul II. All three saw Soviet Communism's moral and structural rot long before most of their peers or followers did.

While Reagan's swagger boosted Americans, it encouraged a cowboy mentality in the White House. The critics' shrillness and their blindness to the Soviet menace polarized foreign policy discourse. Dismissing critics as "wimps," many Reagan aides pooh-poohed constitutional niceties to achieve their boss's objectives. This rogue mentality led them to ignore congressional restrictions on helping the Contras who fought Nicaragua's populist Marxist, Soviet-backed Sandinistas. Similarly, Reagan staffers, led by the charismatic, manipulative superpatriot Colonel Oliver North, pushed hard to free seven American terrorists kidnapped in Lebanon, just a few years after Iran finally freed its American hostages.

Reagan's fierce anti-Communism blinded him to the complexities of the Central American situation and confused him regarding Iran's theocracy, which seemed to him less perverse than godless Communism. The hostages' families' heartrending appeals overly personalized the issue for Reagan. Iran-Contra was the sterile product of this crossbreeding as Reagan's clear, aggressive anti-Communism mixed unhealthily with a sloppy, sentimental approach to Middle East terrorism.

Desperately seeking "a breakthrough" to free the hostages, Reagan approved a series of secret initiatives in 1985 to mollify supposed moderates in Iran. Reagan's aides shipped arms to Iran via Israel, hoping these weapons could be exchanged for the hostages. Eventually, American operatives supplied Iran with 2,008 TOW antitank missiles and tons of spare parts. The terrorists who received money and direction from Tehran released two hostages—but kidnapped others shortly thereafter. Meanwhile, "Field Marshal North"—as Pentagon critics mockingly referred to Reagan's aide Oliver North—diverted profits from the Iranian arms sales to fund the Contras. Such machinations broke the Boland Amendment, the law Congress passed limiting aid to the Contras, while violating Reagan's oft-stated principle not to negotiate with terrorists.

During this same period, Reagan's iconoclasm, shaped by his idiosyncratic faith in his ideology and in the power of personal chemistry, led him to seek a more personal connection with Soviet leaders. Despite his bravado, Reagan paid attention to public opinion. Accusations that he was warmongering stung. His wife Nancy had decided that he should devote his second term to forging his legacy as a peacemaker. The aging Soviet premier Leonid Brezhnev had proved too infirm to respond to Reagan's overture after the assassination attempt. Even though Reagan was America's oldest president ever, he watched two more Soviet premiers emerge, languish, and die. Finally, in 1985 a young, dynamic, fifty-four-year-old reformer named Mikhail Gorbachev became the Soviet leader.

Reagan defied conventional wisdom by meeting Gorbachev in Geneva in November 1985, the first summit in six years. Orchestrating the atmospherics with the care of a Hollywood director, Reagan had a cozy chat with just Gorbachev and two translators by a roaring fireplace in a woody poolhouse next to Lake Geneva. Reagan emerged from his meeting with the

8. President Reagan and Soviet General Secretary Mikhail Gorbachev meet at their first summit in Geneva, Switzerland, November 19, 1985.

surprise announcement that the two would meet again. Reagan took particular delight in disproving the claim that he could not operate without staffers hovering. He also never felt as powerful or self-satisfied as when he succeeded by deploying his tremendous personal charm.

Reagan was surprisingly pragmatic about the Soviets, to the conservatives' chagrin. One grassroots conservative activist, Richard Viguerie, called Reagan a Theodore Roosevelt in reverse: Reagan spoke loudly, but only carried "a small twig," not a big stick. "It would be foolish to believe the leopard will change its spots," Reagan reassured his worried anti-Communist friends including George Murphy. "I think our job is to show him [Gorbachev] he and they will be better off if we make some practical agreements without attempting to convert him to our way of thinking."

As the second-term domestic agenda sputtered, as his administration staggered, the unlikely friendship between Ronald Reagan and Mikhail Gorbachev transformed the world. The greatest events of the 1980s—Communism's collapse and the Cold War's end—vindicated Reagan. Even as he slowed considerably and lost power politically, he proved effective diplomatically.

From the conventional perspective, Reagan appeared inconsistent. At the Reykjavik summit in October 1986 he entertained sweeping proposals, telling Gorbachev, "It would be fine with me if we eliminated all nuclear weapons." Yet this summit, hovering on the edge of a revolutionary breakthrough, collapsed over Reagan's stubborn defense of SDI. Democrats mocked Reagan's faith in this "Star Wars" aerial missile defense system as pie-in-the-sky, Hollywood fantasizing. Reagan had starred as Secret Service agent Bass Bancroft, who protected the "Inertia Projector," a futuristic death ray in the 1940 film *Murder in the Air*. But Reagan's faith in the project stemmed from his faith in America, in science, and in alternatives to the conventional MAD approach. Whatever the science, the Soviet leaders were among the few who believed the missile defense would work. They also learned to take Reagan's commitment to the project very seriously.

In Reykjavik, Gorbachev harangued Reagan about how destabilizing SDI would be. Missile defenses rendered existing missiles useless, inviting more of an arms race. "The meeting is over," Reagan announced abruptly before Gorbachev had even finished, "Let's go, George." As Reagan put on his coat, and a shocked Secretary of State George Shultz prepared to follow, the Soviet premier pleaded, "Can't we do something about this?" Reagan replied: "It's too late." Reporters, Democrats, and allies worried about Reagan's bullheadedness, even as the president averted a crisis wherein American allies might have been unnerved by the sweep of his pacifism.

Shortly after this summit failed, a Lebanese newspaper revealed the Reagan administration's involvement in negotiating for hostages via the Iranians, selling arms to the Iranians and then illegally financing the Contras in Latin America with the profits from these questionable Middle East machinations. The timing was particularly shocking because Reagan, after years of posturing, had finally fought terrorism. In October 1985, Palestinian terrorists hijacked the Italian cruise ship the *Achille Lauro* and murdered an elderly, wheelchair-bound Jewish passenger, Leon Klinghoffer, dumping his body into the sea. The hijackers escaped to Egypt. As the terrorists flew to Tunisia for a hero's welcome from Yasir Arafat and their fellow Palestine Liberation Organization terrorists, Reagan authorized four Navy F-14s to intercept the jet. "You can run, but you can't hide," Reagan boasted after the jet's forced landing in Sicily.

Months later, on April 14, 1986, after Libyan operatives bombed a German disco that American soldiers frequented, America bombed Libya. The raid killed 150 Libyans, including the Libyan dictator Muammar Qaddafi's two-year-old adopted daughter. Europeans condemned the attack. Most Americans applauded their president for finally living up to the Rambo Reagan myth—and for protecting America.

The Iran-Contra news in November 1986 undermined Reagan's standing as an honorable man and a tough leader. Reagan lamented that for the first time the American people did not believe him—and for good reason. His explanations were inconsistent. Ultimately, Reagan avoided impeachment by claiming he was out of touch and possibly incompetent rather than responsible and thus guilty.

As America's scandal investigating machinery kicked into gear, the Democrats' comeback, seizing back a Senate majority in the November 1986 midterm elections, became more significant. Reagan would try to deflect the congressional investigation with his own White House investigation. But the Democrats controlled Congress's investigatory mechanisms—and deployed them to full effect. The political psychodrama culminated with Ollie North's self-serving yet strangely effective testimony before the joint congressional committee. North offered a burst of near-pornographic patriotism that distracted Americans from the scandal's sordid details. Still, all the embarrassing revelations of incompetent diplomacy and illegal chicanery could have terminated a less popular president. A leader less resilient might not have been able to continue the delicate dance with the Soviets while mired in the Iran-Contra morass.

Reagan kept to his two-pronged strategy of seeking peace while defending freedom. In June 1987 Reagan thrilled the world at Germany's Brandenburg Gate, where Soviets had divided the Communist East from the democratic West with the infamous Berlin Wall. Acknowledging the Soviet moves toward "reform and openness," Reagan challenged his rivals: "Mr. Gorbachev, open this gate! Mr. Gorbachev, tear down this wall." Reagan's plea became a great moment of political theater, casting America as a beacon of freedom—and the power knocking down the Soviet Union, even as it imploded, mostly due to internal decay.

Diplomacy's plodding spadework continued amid the flashy rhetorical fireworks. With the real Berlin Wall still standing, Reagan would host Gorbachev half a year later in Washington. This summit provided another opportunity to tear down more symbolic walls between the two great powers.

The president of the United States kept negotiating with the Soviets throughout his nightmarish autumn of 1987, while helping his wife cope with her own illness and her mother's death. When his mother-in-law died, Reagan flew to Phoenix with Nancy, returned to Washington the same day to meet the Soviet foreign minister, then flew back to Phoenix three days later for the funeral—after finalizing the ground-breaking INF agreement with

9. President Reagan urges Mikhail Gorbachev to "tear down this wall" at the Brandenburg Gate, Federal Republic of Germany, June 12, 1987.

the Soviets and scheduling a Washington summit. Despite the president's power, "There was nothing I could do to bring happiness to my wife at a time when she desperately needed it," he mourned.

Reagan hosted the Washington summit in December 1987. "Gorby fever" woud end the scandal-ridden year of "Ollie Mania" on a high note. Gorbachev charmed his American hosts in private parties with glamorous celebrities like Henry Kissinger and Yoko Ono, and by spontaneous bursts of handshaking and back-slapping with smitten citizens. At the summit, the two leaders signed the sweeping treaty eliminating their intermediate-range and shorter-range missiles, feeding Americans' euphoria. Delighted with his achievement, Reagan reassured his conservative comrade William Buckley, saying a few weeks later, "I still think that we are on solid ground on the INF Treaty based on our verification provisions and on the fact that Gorby knows what our response to cheating would be—it's spelled Pershing."

Privately during the summit, the two leaders sparred in a friendly fashion, with Gorbachev wincing as Reagan yet again repeated his "favorite" Russian maxim: "*doverey, no proverey—*trust but verify." The trust was a little strained during one afternoon session, when the president responded to Gorbachev's progress report about his reforms with a tired anecdote about competing students moonlighting as cab drivers. The American cabbie said, "I haven't decided yet," when asked about his educational goals, as the Soviet cabbie admitted, "*They* haven't told me yet."

Even Reagan realized he had overstepped. The episode was kept private initially and was not repeated. Thus, Ronald Reagan's nightmarish 1987 ended on a high note. It was hard to believe, but the saber rattler was looking like a peacemaker; with one year to go, Reagan's long-standing Soviet enemy was offering him political, diplomatic, and historical salvation.

Americans were incredulous, unsure whether to believe this change was real. After hobnobbing with Gorby during the Washington summit, former secretary of state Henry Kissinger published a four-thousand-word essay in *Newsweek* warning against being dazzled by the "euphoria." Ignoring the pacifist and radical streaks in Reagan's ideology, Kissinger declared himself shocked that "This most conservative of postwar presidents seemed bent on ending his term by dismantling the concepts and practices that have shaped Western strategy for four decades."

More than a year later, Kissinger's associate Brent Skowcroft, the National Security Adviser in the new George II. W. Bush administration, remained disturbed that the Reagan administration declared the Cold War over so hastily. Influenced by Kissinger, Scowcroft feared "wishful thinking." Scowcroft believed the "old men of the Politburo" hired Gorbachev to "revitalize" Communism, not end it, making "Gorbachev potentially more dangerous than his predecessors, each of whom, through some aggressive move, had saved the West from the dangers of its own wishful thinking about the Soviet Union before it was too late."

Nevertheless, in hindsight, and to the superficial observer of the time, the Soviet implosion—and the resulting love affair with "Gorby"—progressed quite smoothly. When Reagan visited Moscow in late May 1988, the world was treated to what the historian John Lewis Gaddis would call "the unusual sight of a Soviet general secretary and an American president strolling amiably through Red Square, greeting tourists and bouncing babies in front of Lenin's tomb, while their respective military aides—each carrying the codes needed to launch nuclear missiles at each other's territory—stood discreetly in the background." Reagan used the summit to celebrate American values. The president hosted an elaborate formal "freedom" banquet for Soviet dissidents, human rights activists, Jewish "refuseniks" long blocked from moving to Israel, and oppressed

Pentecostals. Reagan also lectured students at Moscow State University about the beauties of liberty as a bust of the Soviet founder Vladimir Lenin loomed in the background.

Five years after America's leading anti-Communist labeled the Soviets the "evil empire," Ronald Reagan was publicly embracing the leader of world Communism. Reagan explained: Gorbachev is "different than any Russian leader I've met before." Cynics noted, "He is the only one Reagan has met." Conservatives feared Reagan had turned soft. Administration officials insisted, "Ronald Reagan hasn't changed, the Soviets have changed."

Six months later, President Reagan and president-elect Bush hosted Gorbachev at Governors Island in New York Harbor for a farewell summit. Addressing the United Nations, Gorbachev admitted that "Today, the preservation of any kind of 'closed' society is impossible." He then unilaterally announced reductions in Soviet forces of a half million soldiers and ten thousand tanks.

Nevertheless, Reagan was surprisingly cautious about the Soviet Union in his farewell address. He seemed to be positioning as much for "plausible deniability" in case relations cooled as for bragging rights in case the Cold War ended. Reagan admitted, "Nothing is less free than pure communism." Still, he justified the "new closeness" because "we're basing our actions not on words but deeds," such as the end to the Soviets' occupation of neighboring Afghanistan. Preempting the historians and critics who would mock his previous record as a skeptic, Reagan contrasted his tough-minded approach, which had yielded results with the détente of the 1970s and which was "based not on actions but promises." Reagan made sure to "wish" President Gorbachev "well" and reiterated his favorite formula yet again: "trust but verify." By contrast, on his last day in office, George H. W. Bush's Inauguration Day, 1989, a more ebullient Reagan boldly declared "the Cold War is over."

President George H. W. Bush changed the dynamic. Reagan balanced his natural tendency toward celebratory bombast with his long-standing hatred of Communism. Bush's WASPish fear of gloating reinforced his instincts toward secrecy and caution. Reagan often spoke in bold colors that sometimes clashed; Bush's overlapping shades of gray often verged on the incoherent. Bush's own secretary of state James Baker would agree that the administration's initial "strategic review" of foreign policy was "neither truly strategic nor a proper review" and resulted in "mush."

Many forces triggered the Soviet Union's collapse as the Cold War ended surprisingly peacefully. Still, Ronald Reagan was not just in the right place at the right time. He was the right man in the right place at the right time. His radical openness to summit-level diplomacy and to eliminating all nuclear weapons, tempered by his insistence on rebuilding America's military and seeking an effective missile defense, worked. Mikhail Gorbachev found a partner, not just an adversary. But Gorbachev also found a rival, not simply a patsy. Reagan knew his conservative allies would trust no agreement with the Soviets, while his liberal critics were tempted to rush into any kind of agreement. By striking the middle path that he did, Reagan accelerated the process, making Mikhail Gorbachev relaxed enough not to mobilize forces or unleash violence to prop up the ailing Soviet regime. As he triumphed, Reagan saw a softer, more reasonable, more human face to the Soviet monolith he had fought so tenaciously for decades.

Chapter 7
Did the Reagan revolution succeed or fail?

Few would have dared predict that the Soviet Communists would give Ronald Reagan his greatest success in office—and grand finale—as the fizzling of the Cold War upstaged the Iran-Contra scandal and the 1987 stock market swoon. Few would have dared predict when Reagan entered office amid astronomical interest rates and growing unemployment that the American economy would boom soon. Few would have dared predict that America was ready, after the despair of the 1970s, to delight in the patriotism of the 1980s. In the great presidential sweepstakes, wherein Americans blame or praise chief executives for what happened on their watch, Reagan therefore earned bragging rights for bringing peace, prosperity, and patriotism—although the real story is more complex.

Those triple triumphs, even if they were completely attributable to Reagan and were not accompanied by baggage such as the gargantuan defense buildup, huge budget deficit, and the growing income gap, beg the question of the Reagan Revolution's success. The Reagan Revolution was a more ambitious enterprise. Ronald Reagan entered office promising to cut taxes, which he did, deregulate, which he did partially, and shrink big government, which he failed to do. He also promised to rebuild the American military, which he did, defeat the Soviet Union, which he did partially, and resurrect American values by undoing the worst excesses of the 1960s and 1970s, which he also failed to do. Perhaps Reagan's most singular short-term success was the confidence, patriotism, and sense of pride he personified and helped bring back to America. Perhaps his great long-term success was in injecting ideas and individuals who would mainstream conservatism and reorient America.

The Reagan Revolution also has to be judged more objectively, on its accomplishments, not simply by its own ambitions. There, the record is more mixed—and contentious. Without rehashing the 1980s' partisanship or triggering the many arguments from those years that continue, we can begin weighing the Reagan Revolution's economic, political, cultural, ideological, and diplomatic legacies. Most Americans felt pretty good about Reagan and the 1980s. But great leaders make enemies as well as friends. Those who felt ignored or marginalized, including

10. President Ronald Reagan and First Lady Nancy Reagan celebrating the rededication and centennial of the Statue of Liberty, New York City, July 4, 1986.

feminists, African Americans, gays, union activists, and intellectuals, felt deeply rejected. Ronald Reagan deserves credit for reviving pride in the red, white, and blue, but his style and stands let too many Americans believe they were irrevocably split into warring camps of what later became known as the red versus the blue.

In 1981, *Parade* magazine asked Ronald Reagan for his thoughts about the Fourth of July. In his distinctive scrawl, the new president wrote out a nostalgic vignette about how much he and others who "grew up in the small towns of the Midwest" looked forward to the Fourth—"I remember it as a day almost as long anticipated as Christmas." Reagan's father would scrape together "what he felt he could afford to see go up in smoke & flame." Responsible enough to note that "we are better off now that fireworks are largely handled by professionals," Reagan could barely contain his childlike glee as he remembered "the thrill never to be forgotten in seeing a tin can blown 30 f[ee]t in the air by a giant 'cracker'—giant meaning it was about 4 inches long."

Having evoked a bygone America, Reagan then launched into his ideological lesson. "Somewhere in our growing up we began to be aware of the meaning of the day and with that awareness came the birth of patriotism," he wrote. "Ours was a revolution that changed the very concept of gov[ernmen]t. Let the 4th of July always be a reminder that here in this land for the 1st time it was decided that man is born with certain God given rights; that gov[ernmen]t is only a convenience created and managed by the people with no power of its own except those voluntarily granted to it by the people." This 381-word prose poem was Reagan's entirely. He wrote most of it in one sitting. Reagan made less than a dozen modifications to his first draft.

Assessments of Ronald Reagan often bog down in confusion over two competing dimensions of his identity, the ideologue and the showman. Ronald Reagan truly was a believer. More than most modern presidents, he had a clear ideological vision. He entered politics as a crusader, a man with a mission. He never abandoned the vision, even if he compromised pragmatically on occasion.

Ronald Reagan was also a showman. He saw politics as an extension of his experiences as an actor, a General Electric shill, and a Las Vegas emcee. He quipped that he could not imagine anyone serving as governor—or president—who *hadn't* been in show business. A shameless crowd-pleaser, he was particularly sensitive to audience response, as both a performer and a politician.

The paradox of his political persona helped account for the success of his presidency. Without the ideological grounding, he would have been a political will-o'-the-wisp, captive to applause meters greeting "the line of the day" his aides selected every morning. Without the showmanship, he would have been too fanatic, unwilling to make the compromises with reality—and public sensibilities—needed to govern effectively.

This creative tension between preaching and pandering, between hewing the line and wooing the people, helps explain his two greatest substantive successes. In managing the economy, Reagan's small government ideology helped free America from the ever-expanding governmental obligations and ever-growing strands of bureaucratic red tape that burdened and strangled the economy in the 1970s. Demonstrating his brute political intelligence, former president Richard Nixon told William F. Buckley Jr. in 1982 that if Reagan "licks inflation, he'll be a national hero." Reagan did—and he was.

But Reagan's sensitive political antennae—along with his lingering love for Franklin Roosevelt—stopped him from dismantling the welfare state and led him to many compromises that slowed the rate of governmental growth rather than actually shrinking the government. With the Soviets, Reagan's anti-Communist ideology helped him see past his experts' opinions and recognize the internal weaknesses afflicting America's rivals. At the same time, his desire to be lionized—along with his pacifist streak—led him to respond to Gorbachev's unexpected overtures—and frequently bold proposals.

In achieving peace and prosperity, Ronald Reagan taught conservatives how to wield power—and expand the presidency. Since the New Deal, America's conservatives had feared presidential power, linking it to big government. With Ronald Reagan, conservatives tasted power—and liked it. The expanded presidency became, in theory, a counterweight against the Congress, the courts and the bureaucracy, checking liberal expansionism. In fact, the Reagan presidency deployed presidential and governmental power in various sometimes contradictory ways, not always limiting government but usually aggrandizing the president. Thanks to Reagan, the presidential superhero no longer had to be a liberal growing the government but could be a conservative trying to tame it.

In reviving American patriotism and helping restore American nationalism, his third great success, Reagan's sense of the dramatic meshed with his worldview. Reagan believed in America. His fellow Americans' reluctance to take pride in their country offended him. Reagan's narrative emphasized how America in the 1960s and 1970s lost its way, how the recession of 1981/82 reflected the necessary readjustment, but then, poof, Reagan's policies paid off, creating Morning in America.

On one level, the red, white, and blue bunting framing so many speeches, and Reagan's patriotic odes to America, reflected a resurgence of American patriotism, helping Americans express their love of their country. But Reagan's conservative ideology and all-American showmanship helped reconstitute Americans' collective identity too. This shift was not just about celebrating America, it was about rediscovering faith in America. Reagan's

American nationalism, even as leading intellectuals mocked it, buoyed the country, offering a necessary corrective to the negativism of the 1960s and 1970s.

It is easy now to be glib about Ronald Reagan's restoration of Americans' faith in themselves and his related accomplishment of putting liberalism on the defensive. But underestimating those achievements reflects how much Reagan changed America. Back when Reagan was shifting careers from acting to politics in the early 1960s, many mainstream academics and politicians deemed liberalism the *only* American ideology. Post–New Deal liberalism celebrated the government as the central vehicle for achieving social justice while valuing the collective over the individual. As a result, millions of Americans, and especially America's leading writers, teachers, journalists, and politicians, believed that taxes were a force for good, labor unions were virtuous, and big government reflected a society's big-hearted aspirations. Marxism itself was remarkably popular, with many even turning a blind eye to Soviet and Maoist Chinese oppression in appreciation of Communism's noble quest for the greatest good.

Reagan shook twentieth-century America's ideological foundations. Summoning up a prophetic wrath against the evils of Communism, tapping a wellspring of faith in American values, and leavening it all with humorous asides referring to liberalism as "the L word" and mocking Communists as bureaucratic clods, Reagan changed the conversation. Taxes became, at best, a necessary evil, at worst, government's great sin against individual initiative. Marxism became passé as Communism collapsed. And labor unions became better known for their corrupt pension funds, strong-arm tactics, and strikes against the public good than their contribution to justice for workers.

More broadly, Reagan's presidency rested on a grand bargain he made with the American people. It was not easy to be a crowd-pleasing ideologue or a conservative revolutionary. Reagan's desire for popularity and respect for the status quo repeatedly trumped his desire for change and his more radical vision. His implicit bargain with constituents kept him singing a song of transformation without making too many demands for implementation.

This covenant led Reagan to raise taxes when faced with huge deficits, maintain the seven most basic government grants to the needy, and preserve more of the governing status quo than most friends and rivals expected. This covenant also extended to the cultural realm—and helps explain the disconnect between Reagan's traditional rhetoric and the way the 1980s legitimized, mainstreamed, and often institutionalized much of the 1960s' revolution. President Reagan was not Governor Reagan. As governor, Reagan picked many more fights with liberals—and fought the forces transforming American society more aggressively—than he did as president.

The conservatives' complaints were justified. Reagan did little to advance what they called their "abc agenda"—against abortion, busing, and crime. The culture wars raged, sometimes fueled by Reagan operatives such as William Bennett, his secretary of education. Yet the president ducked if the cultural issues became too heated. When Reagan retired, abortion remained legal, students still were being bused out of their neighborhoods to integrate schools, and the crime rate remained inexcusably high.

In the ultimate expression of his caution—and this covenant— Reagan started a tradition of broadcasting a message to the annual Right to Life protest in Washington, without actually appearing. This compromise let him rally the religious Right without being defined by a picture that would make him appear too radical for John Q. Public. The result, in many ways, was the Reagan Reconciliation, as feminism, environmentalism, the sexual revolution, civil rights, gay liberation, even sixties-style informality became woven into America's social and ideological fabric. Some of the movements lost their edge, but they gained respectability and reach.

Reagan's reluctance to fight the forces that were liberalizing the country also stopped him from tackling what we could call the conservative contradiction: the capitalism and consumerism he helped unleash threatened to destroy the ideals he seemed to most cherish. Reagan's preaching conjured up images of a renewed American community. He and his fellow conservatives spoke of an old-fashioned neighborliness, of a sense of altruism, of enduring American values.

Reagan's optimism was a great gift to conservatism. Tapping into Americans' traditional, positive, can-do spirit, he moved the Right from its sourpuss solitude, lamenting America's decline with the consistency but unpopularity of the righteous, into the populist mainstream. Reflecting his New Deal roots, Reagan made modern conservatism more progressive, more constructive, than earlier versions associated with Barry Goldwater's tartness, Joe McCarthy's harshness, and Herbert Hoover's tightfistedness.

Reagan was correct. There was much to celebrate. America remained one of the modern world's great marvels. Millions of immigrants continued flocking to America, finding liberation in the land of the free and the home of the brave. Tens of millions of Americans thrived, privileged to live in one of the freest, wealthiest, most humane, most generous, most big-hearted, and most successful collective enterprises in history. Beyond all the technological, pharmacological, cultural, and artistic miracles produced annually, Americans remained among the most generous people on earth. In 2006, decades into the Reagan Revolution, Professor Arthur Brooks would note that three of four American families donated money annually, with average giving per household having nearly tripled since World War II. More than half of American families volunteered time for both secular and religious causes—with American rates of giving time and money surpassing those of European countries and Canada.

Nevertheless, all this optimism, all these celebrations, all the good works, coexisted uncomfortably with a growing pessimism about American society and a gnawing fear of decline. At their grimmest, Reagan and his conservative supporters feared modern America's no-holds-barred, anything-goes culture. Reagan's rejected Supreme Court nominee Robert Bork would write a jeremiad in 1996 against the superficialities and barbarities of popular culture called *Slouching toward Gomorrah*. Allan Bloom, an obscure University of Chicago academic, would become a modern conservative icon with his best-selling 1987 tirade against rock music and his students' "nice" but empty values in *The Closing of the American Mind*. But the conservative contradiction prevented Reagan—and most conservatives—from taking responsibility for their collective roles in making America a more selfish and superficial nation.

The peculiar form of consumer-oriented capitalism that Reagan helped resurrect proved particularly toxic for the old-fashioned values Reagan wanted to protect. In Reagan's America, the entrepreneurial ethos fed a prosperity, a showiness, and an individualism that undermined traditional values and Americans' sense of community. While economists still argue about just how widely the prosperity was distributed, and what inequities, if any, resulted, most social critics agree that Americans' standards for judging each other and themselves became distorted. Eighties America, while a wealthy country, was also a country of people working harder than ever, and spending more and more money on ever larger houses, ever fancier clothes, ever more expensive meals. Americans risked gorging on the feast of freedom Reagan helped unleash.

Coverage making the rich famous for their lifestyles fueled an envy epidemic. A 1980s aesthetic took hold, reflecting the decade's prosperity with the glint of chromium, the glow of neon, the gleam of bold colors. Corporate men and women dressed in "power suits," confusing money, power, and virtue.

While *New York Times* editorials denounced American excess, the paper ran front-page stories about lavish living that distorted people's notions of what they "needed" or what was "normal." Businessmen like Lee Iacocca, the chairman of Chrysler, and Donald Trump, the real estate mogul, became celebrities, role models, and standards by which people judged their own lives— and spending habits. Studies showed that most Americans, even millionaires, defined their notions of material comfort one or two rungs higher than their own financial level. The modern "rat race" had become an exhausting Sisyphean sprint up the never-ending spending stairway.

As what people perceived to be their "needs" escalated, selfishness and materialism frequently trumped idealism and altruism. In the tradition of modern presidents who dodged difficult choices, Reagan's revived nationalism tended to emphasize swagger and self-satisfaction over self-sacrifice. The assault on regulation and on government's credibility helped feed a Wild West mentality on Wall Street—and helped miss some of the overly abstract and risky practices—that would trigger 2008's financial meltdown. Most Americans had enough money to overspend on some things. And it cost nothing to be envious or money-hungry. In 1967, as baby boomer idealism peaked, 40 percent of college freshmen in one poll assessing various life goals most valued being rich; 80 percent sought a meaningful philosophy of life; twenty years later, 80 percent desired wealth, only 40 percent mentioned seeking meaning as a priority.

Owning so many things, Americans lacked moorings. Money served as a social solvent, while lubricating arrivistes' climb to the top. A hard-driving, high-earning, big-spending nation pushed the enlightenment legacies of emancipation and individualism to their logical—and often illogical—extremes. The twentieth century was a centrifugal century. Urbanization, individuation, automation, media penetration, mobility, prosperity, consumerism, and the rights revolution developed over decades. The resulting "radical individualism," the sociologist Robert Bellah explained, created a largely "negative" process of "giving birth to oneself" by "breaking free from family, community, and inherited ideas." A nation of disconnected searchers, divorced from traditional "sources of authority, duty and moral example," hoped to "find themselves."

All these goodies, all the freedoms, did not produce happier children or adults. As American leisure culture became a carnival of sensual delights, this pleasure addiction often brought individual and mass misery. Experts tracked epidemics of child abuse, child poverty, juvenile delinquency, teenage depression, teenage suicide, teenage alcoholism, and teenage drug abuse. Even as the nation's collective bill for psychological services and psychiatric drugs soared, millions of individuals' morale sagged.

Within corporations, Darwinian pressure to survive encouraged cost-cutting and corner-cutting. On Wall Street, the push to make money culminated in waves of white-collar scandals, as well-dressed masters of the universe did the ritualized perp walk with their expensive Armani suit jackets draped over their handcuffs. Community spirit, professional ethics, and respect for the law suffered amid overbilling, conflicts-of-interest, and tax evasion. Jobs became less secure and more stressful. The real-life corporate version of the hot new video game Pac-Man had corporate raiders buying out companies, stripping them of assets, and turning a quick profit—often at the workers' expense. Mass firings and the constant downsizing undermined the corporate sense of loyalty and community.

Similarly, the push for privatization at the federal, state, and local levels also weakened the communal sense of interconnectedness and accountability. The legitimate conservative critique of many lumbering government bureaucracies fed an unhealthy retreat from public structures and public investment. When entrepreneurs like Donald Trump took responsibility for renovating Central Park's skating rink, the public benefitted in the short term but with sobering long-term costs. The lost faith in the government fueled the flight to corporate solutions, blinding many to big business's excesses. The rise of gated communities with private police, private sanitation, and walls preserving members' privacy symbolized this shift from the public to the private, from equitable solutions for all to customized solutions for the rich. The push to privatize other communal structures, such as prisons, raised thorny philosophical and legal questions about which services the state could outsource, and on what basis the government deputized private corporations to perform police and other community functions.

Tragically, both the Left and the Right approached the problems myopically, polemically. Blinded by their critique of the Left, Ronald Reagan and most conservatives proved unable to connect the dots between the capitalist resurgence they celebrated and the cultural upheaval they mourned. They failed to see how many of the policies they implemented and the corporate practices they applauded neutralized or undermined many traditional values and structures. They often used patriotism, morality, and faith as blinders to avoid seeing problems and barriers to obstruct solutions. At the same time, the liberal tendency to reduce so many political and social questions to questions of "rights" furthered the retreat from the "us" to the "I." The rise of identity politics emphasized ethnic and racial communities at the cost of a broader sense of national community, just as the emphasis on "my rights" eroded individuals' sense of communal responsibility. Blinded, for their part, by their fury against the Right, too many on the left allowed conservatives to monopolize discussions about patriotism, morality, and religion. This abdication marked a dangerous tendency to view the flag, family, and faith as belonging to right-wing partisans rather than the nation's common heritage.

Modern Western society's great gift, freedom, came with costs that had to be managed. "Is it possible that we could become citizens again and together seek the common good in the post-industrial, postmodern age?" the sociologist Robert Bellah and his colleagues asked in 1985's surprise bestseller *Habits of the Heart.* "Freedom is a moral accomplishment," the British theologian Jonathan Sacks would write in *The Politics of Hope* in 1997, illustrating that the problem was Western, not just American. "It needs strong families, cohesive institutions, habits of civility and law-abidingness, and a widely diffused sense of fellow-feeling.... When moral language breaks down—as it has broken down—much else is at risk, including freedom itself."

This breakdown was not simply the fault of the dreaded "liberals" or "conservatives." America's crisis as the 1980s ended was partially a joint accomplishment—and partially independent of the politicians, no matter what their ideology. Many of the most unnerving social and cultural changes resulted from postwar America's extraordinary expansion of freedom. Much of the economic dislocation reflected America's transition from an industrial economy to a service, consumer-oriented, and high-tech economy. And the persistence of racism, poverty, and crime revealed the intractability of these problems.

Democrats—and most historians—were quick to blame all this on Reagan. But the historian William Leuchtenburg saw in the 1920s the "Perils of Prosperity." Academics have long been ambivalent about the good times, preferring the Spartan drama of depression and war to the abandon of boom times. Bill Clinton's roaring 1990s showed that cultural excess was not solely a Republican affliction; Democrats could be equally indulgent. That so many observers blame him for this broader

phenomenon—or believed he could somehow change it—reflects
Ronald Reagan's outsized impact on his times

The presidential ratings game, like the stock market, can
fluctuate wildly. The twenty-first century began with Ronald
Reagan's reputation on the upswing. Even if his revolution was
more moderate than he hoped, even if his proposed solutions were
less effective or global than he believed, he was a significant and
surprisingly successful president. The Reagan Revolution, such
as it was, for all its limitations and excesses, provided a valuable
mid-course correction to Lyndon Johnson's Great Society.
Americans—and their leaders—needed to remember that
bureaucracy could not solve every problem. Americans—and
some of their leaders—needed to remember the country's strengths
as well as its weaknesses. Certainly, Reagan was lucky. The
economy was ready to boom; the Soviets were ready to crumble.
But his revolution accomplished as much as it did—and
resonated for the next few decades—because Reagan was enough
of a believer to have a bottom-line yet enough of a showman to
know when to compromise, and how important it was to please
his audience, the American people.

Chapter 8

When did the Reagan revolution end?

On June 5, 2004, just as the presidential campaign between Senator John Kerry and President George W. Bush was heating up, Ronald Reagan died. Reagan was ninety-three and had receded from public view over the previous decade as his Alzheimer's disease advanced. Yet, surprisingly, the week of eulogies culminating in Reagan's funeral on June 11, 2004, triggered a national outpouring of emotion. Democrats who had built their careers campaigning against the man and his legacy praised him as an optimistic patriot who helped win the Cold War. Conservatives who had grumbled about Reagan's moderation during his tenure tearfully embraced him as their hero.

There is a commendable American tendency to eulogize presidents in a gracious nonpartisan manner. Senator Richard Nixon mocked Harry Truman as soft on Communism and surrounded by corrupt cronies during the 1952 campaign, but President Nixon presided with dignity over Truman's funeral twenty years later. In 1974 a young Bill Clinton cheered his girlfriend, Hillary Rodham, for helping the House of Representatives Judiciary Committee seek Richard Nixon's impeachment. Nevertheless, in 1994 President Clinton delivered a moving eulogy at Nixon's funeral.

Still, the posthumous praise of Ronald Reagan exceeded the usual mourning rituals for American statesmen. The week-long focus on Reagan and his legacy reinforced Reaganites' claim that his was a monumental presidency. The heartfelt bipartisan tributes illustrated that, in some ways, the Reagan Revolution—as constrained as it was in the 1980s—continued to shape America into the twenty-first century.

Sometimes, doctors can inject contrasting dyes into their patients' bloodstreams or organs to track particular influences, be they malignant or benign. Historians can only envy such scientific precision. Still, it is worth imagining what would appear if a red-white-and-blue colored dye injected into daily American life could track Reaganism's influence since Ronald and Nancy Reagan took their farewell helicopter ride from the Capitol in January 1989.

Whatever ambivalence George Herbert Walker Bush may have had regarding his predecessor, the first Bush administration was in many ways Reagan's third term. Many analysts attributed Bush's come-from-behind victory over Governor Michael Dukakis to the continuing potency of Reagan's magic. Less loftily, Reaganite operatives like Lee Atwater brought their aggressive, experienced, often ideological edge to the campaign. Democrats in 1988 seemed as flummoxed as they did when mounting Walter Mondale's campaign against Reagan's reelection in 1984.

At his inauguration, George H. W. Bush began his delicate dance, trying to distinguish himself from Reagan without disrespecting Reagan. Bush began by thanking the retiring president formally and broadly—but generically and perfunctorily—for "the wonderful things that you have done for America." However, as Bush spoke, even as he emphasized his "kinder, gentler" approach, Reaganism's echoes resonated loudly. Bush's insistence that "We know what works: Freedom works. We know what's right: Freedom is right," embraced Reaganesque capitalism—and anti-Communism. Bush's refusal to rely on "public money alone" to solve social and political problems championed Reagan's anti-government stance. And Bush shared Reagan's populist faith in the people when he claimed that "the wisest thing of all" was to "turn to the only resource we have that in times of need always grows—the goodness and the courage of the American people."

In governing, Bush struggled with many of the items that Reagan had placed on the national agenda. Bush's Reaganesque pledge—"No new taxes"—would haunt him, when he was finally forced, as Reagan had been, to raise revenues due to the continuing, Reagan-fueled, budget deficits. Bush was even less inclined than Reagan to be a social crusader or generate intense controversy. Bush continually disappointed conservatives by following Reagan's tradition of piping in greetings to the "right to life" movement rally and doing little to stop the social and cultural revolutions changing—conservatives said "ruining"—America.

Bush paid a steep political price for the continuing fallout from Reagan's two terms in office. A recession hit, which many reporters deemed to be the natural corrective to Reaganomics. In addition to the dollars and cents of the economy, the economic downturn satisfied the liberal cosmology, whereby America needed to suffer for enjoying so much prosperity.

Bush's dislike for the Reagan model of leadership muted America's response when Soviet Communism finally fell. Bush was shrewd in not wanting to gloat, fearing that too much American delirium might trigger a Soviet backlash. But his caution deprived the American people of a defining victory moment. Bush's prudence appeared plodding and amoral when he abandoned the Chinese student protesters crushed by their government during the spring 1989 Tiananmen Square protests. The students took the Statue of Liberty as a model, but Bush was no "freedom man"; he failed the test rhetorically and diplomatically.

Bush's controversial nomination of Clarence Thomas to the Supreme Court also had many Reagan resonances. Thomas was a model Reaganaut. He and other conservative intellectuals learned how to turn the federal bureaucracy against itself, in his case by fighting affirmative action rather than expanding it when leading the Equal Employment Opportunity Commission. An African American, Thomas also represented the wave of young blacks who entered professions like law and medicine, and advanced thanks to affirmative action—whether they endorsed the policy or not. And Bush's nomination of this ideologue reflected an attempt to extend Ronald Reagan's judicial revolution, perhaps the most effective flank in Reagan's multidimensional assault on the Great Society.

The public fight when Thomas's former assistant Anita Hill accused him of sexual harassment incorporated even more Reagan-era themes. As a female black law professor, Anita Hill represented the achievements of feminism and the civil rights movement since the 1980s, along with the growing frustrations. That millions debated what constituted sexual harassment showed how the 1980s' Reagan Reconciliation mainstreamed and integrated certain ideas considered radical before the 1960s. The splashy, flashy, trashy, exceedingly public nature of the televised clash when Professor Hill accused Judge Thomas of inappropriate and vulgar advances furthered the coarsening of pop culture and the let-it-all-hang-out televised populism that characterized 1980s' political culture.

Finally, the 1992 African American riots in Los Angeles added a violent note to this apparent anti-Reagan backlash, harnessing the frustrations of the post-Reagan recession with some of the racial demons the Hill-Thomas hearings had stirred. Even Democrats who blamed Reaganism for what some called the insurrection in Ronald Reagan's California backyard still had to acknowledge that the backlash itself reflected the Reagan years' transformative impact.

The Democratic presidential candidate in 1992 rode to the White House on the wings of the anti-Reagan backlash. In his triumphal campaign, Bill Clinton cleverly put George Bush's less popular, less entrancing brand on defining Reagan programs and accomplishments. Rarely mentioning Reagan's name, Clinton frequently bashed the 1980s as a time of "economic disaster," of America's rich getting richer, of America going from "the world's largest creditor to being the world's largest debtor. The stock market tripled, but wages went down." Clinton also deemed Reaganomics immoral, blasting Republicans as the party of junk bonds, corporate raiders, and Wall Street cheats. Clinton worried that in business schools such as the University of Pennsylvania's Wharton School, "by 1987, the year the stock market crashed, 25% of the graduating class was going into investment banking—a quarter of the best graduates at one of America's top business schools pursuing high incomes in high finance rather than in the apparently less glamorous work of creating jobs, goods and services to make America richer."

Surprisingly, President Clinton inched closer to the Reaganite agenda than candidate Clinton ever imagined. Shortly after defeating George Bush, Clinton assured the NBC news reporter Andrea Mitchell that he would fulfill his promise to integrate gays into the military. This response was honest, principled, but politically explosive. The controversy highlighted Clinton's distance from military culture, stirred moderate suspicions that Clinton was more radical than he admitted, and contrasted with Reagan's approach of playing to the center, confident that his core supporters had nowhere to go. Eventually, Clinton backtracked. In a different context, his "don't ask, don't tell" policy could have appeared to be progress for gays rather than a pathetic fig leaf covering up a betrayal by a politician many gays supported enthusiastically.

This early gays-in-the-military fiasco, combined with Clinton's failure to enact his sweeping health care reform, propelled

Clinton toward more Reaganesque positions. In the 1994 midterm elections, Republicans achieved a victory that had eluded them in the 1980s. They captured the House of Representatives for the first time since the Eisenhower era forty years earlier.

Two years after a string of Republican repudiations culminated with George Bush's defeat, Republicans were resurgent. The new Speaker of the House and Republican point man, Newt Gingrich, had ambitious plans to govern as a conservative ideologue less accommodating than Reagan. Gingrich and his Republicans offered a "Contract with America" promising to complete the revolution Reagan never fully implemented. The contract promised a balanced budget, tax cuts, welfare limits, support for families, tough anti-crime provisions, distance from any kind of United Nations supervision of American troops, limits on civil suits, congressional reform, and term limits.

Cowed, anxious to secure re-election, President Clinton tacked right. He had already proven to be more fiscally responsible than Reagan himself, achieving a balanced budget, then a budget surplus—achievements that eluded the Republican revolutionary. Clinton declared in his 1996 State of the Union address that the "era of big government is over." He passed a tough welfare reform bill that appalled many of his own White House staffers and depressed the First Lady Hillary Clinton. Coached by his political guru Dick Morris, Clinton ran for re-election as "the good father," reassuring traditionalists with cultural Band-Aids, proposing the V-chip in televisions to limit children's access to inappropriate programs, and school uniforms to encourage discipline.

Stylistically, Clinton mimicked Reagan too. Clinton learned from Reagan the art of spin and the craft of big picture governing. Just as Reagan's sweeping vision and lyrical speeches limited the damage from his many verbal gaffes and minor missteps, Clinton's popular message helped protect him from the many scandals his indiscreet behavior caused. Ultimately, Clinton survived the Monica Lewinsky scandal in ways that paralleled Reagan's survival despite Iran-Contra.

Like Reagan, Clinton became the peace and prosperity president. Democrats had a harder time mocking Reagan in retrospect as their party became the party of the baby boomers' big economic boom. Fewer Democrats could attribute the inequitable distribution of income that emerged to Reagan, as the big bucks raked in by investment bankers and innovative entrepreneurs became as characteristic of the Clinton 1990s as they were of the Reagan 1980s.

Clinton's successor, George W. Bush, also confounded expectations. The second President Bush distanced himself from the first Bush presidency to embrace Reagan as a political model. Bush's "compassionate conservatism" first sounded like a critique of Reaganite conservatism, implying that the original lacked mercy. But Bush emphasized the conservatism more than the compassion.

In a newly center-right nation, George W. Bush's conservatism was tactical. He attributed his father's defeat in 1992 to the alienated conservative base. Karl Rove, the new president's adviser, believed the 2000 election had been so close because 4 to 5 million conservative Republican evangelical voters chose to stay home rather than voting for another Bush. Rove pushed George W. Bush to out-Reagan Reagan, playing to the Right to mobilize those voters in 2004.

Bush's narrow Electoral College victory and his fragile political footing highlighted a paradoxical result of the Reagan Revolution. Reagan resurrected the center, reviving a broad sense of patriotism and American nationalism. But especially during the Bill Clinton and George W. Bush presidencies, many Americans feared their nation was dysfunctionally polarized between the so-called "red" pro-Reagan states and the more cosmopolitan, progressive, "blue" states.

Reagan helped redraw America's electoral map, uniting pro-Republican western states with the once solidly Democratic South. Many of the wedge issues separating "red" from "blue" were the building blocks of the Reagan platform. "Red" Americans favored cutting taxes, continuing to deregulate, outlawing abortion, ending affirmative action, punishing criminals harshly, limiting multilateralism, boosting the military, and managing the effects of the sexual revolution. But the paradox of the Reagan Revolution continued. The Electoral College map exaggerated the differences between the red and the blue states and obscured the warring impulses within so many Americans. The United States would not have had the high divorce rates, abortion rates, crime rates, or governmental growth rates if Americans lived as their states voted. Many red state Americans led far more "liberal" lives and many blue state Americans led far more traditional lives than the media caricatures suggested. Similarly, farmers and entrepreneurs, big business leaders and small business owners overlooked whatever governmental goodies they received when discussions turned toward cutting budgets and ending government support for programs servicing others.

The traumatic terrorist attacks on September 11, 2001, barely eight months into the Bush presidency, further tied George W. Bush to Ronald Reagan's legacy. Combining the Reagan-Clinton approach of big picture governance, learning from Reagan's focus on anti-Communism, George W. Bush devoted his presidency to prosecuting the war on terror. Unfortunately, President Bush frequently reduced Reagan's nuanced, multidimensional strategy to a heavy-handed, one-dimensional strategy.

Bush romanticized Reagan as more of a swashbuckler than he actually had been. Reagan "didn't say, 'Well, Mr. Gorbachev, would you take the top three bricks off the wall," Bush explained in a May 2002 interview about Reagan's legacy. "He said, tear it all down." Actually, Reagan's actions were more temperate than his rhetoric. Reagan never tried knocking down the Berlin Wall, and he negotiated with Mikhail Gorbachev for two years before making his pronouncement.

Some observers argued that even though Bush's swagger seemed to be channeling Ronald Reagan, September 11 marked the end of the Reagan era. The emergence of terrorism as America's central national security issue and the monstrous Bush-era deficits steered the country away from the Reaganesque concerns about shrinking big government and defeating Communism. Many Democrats pointed to the financial crash of 2008 as not just the end but the repudiation of the Reagan era. Others pointed to March 2003, when the United States invaded Iraq, as the final end point. Still others insisted that it was November 2006, when the voters rejected so many Republican Congress members as they returned the House of Representatives to Democratic control, that the era of the Republican fight against big government finally seemed finished. And yet, during the 2008 campaign, Ronald Reagan was not only the most frequently invoked modern politician among Republicans, Senator Barack Obama admired Reagan's commitment to pursuing his particular vision, no matter how wrongheaded.

Historians need more distance from the early part of the twenty-first century before it becomes clearer when the Reagan epoch ended, and what needs to be emphasized in its stead. Still, Americans live in a Reaganized America and can find traces of that contrasting red, white, and blue dye in so much of American public life—and even in Americans' private lives.

Perhaps the best way to appreciate Reagan's impact—and continuing relevance in today's Reaganized America—is to join the millions of tourists who visit Washington, DC. Today, the capital's airport is called "Ronald Reagan Washington National Airport." The airport outgrew its original 1941 Art Deco main terminal and added terminals with huge lattice-covered ceilings that evoke 1980s architecture. Continuing the retail revolution that began under Reagan, the airport feels like a shopping mall, with many franchised shops and fast-food chains dominating the food courts.

Driving into the city from the airport's location in Arlington, Virginia, over the Fourteenth Street Bridge, visitors can see the largest building in Washington, with 3.1 million square feet of space devoted to its unique mix of public and private tenants. The Ronald Reagan Building and International Trade Center opened in 1998 on what had been a parking lot. The building was part of the resurrection of Pennsylvania Avenue, which reflected the 1980s' broader urban gentrification trends. In an ironic tribute to the man who wanted to shrink government but left gargantuan deficits, when the U.S. General Services Administration finished building the Ronald Reagan building, its $768 million price tag made it the most expensive building the government had ever built at the time.

Two blocks over is the most famous address in America, 1600 Pennsylvania Avenue. While the process began with Theodore Roosevelt and Franklin Roosevelt, Ronald Reagan certainly played a role in making the White House loom so large in the American popular imagination. Reagan and his people taught their successors how to use the White House as the great, all-American stage set, offering the perfect backdrop for the bully pulpit. They helped perfect the politics of sound bites and spin that has entertained, informed, alienated, and frustrated a generation of Americans already. Fears of big government did not extend to fears of a powerful presidency. The Reagan era helped push the scales in the constant balance between Congress and the executive toward 1600 Pennsylvania Avenue.

In the West Wing and the Oval Office, where the president and key staffers work, the daily agenda remains filled with Reagan-era concerns. The constant pressure to cut taxes, the fear of big bureaucratic Great Society programs even after the financial meltdown, the questions about how and what to regulate after two decades of deregulation, the renewed respect for military prerogatives—and budget requests—all bear Ronald Reagan's fingerprints. Similarly, throughout the federal bureaucracy, the ideological diversity of staffers represents a dramatic break from pre-1980 days, when conservatives had more or less abdicated the executive branch to Franklin Roosevelt's New Dealers, John Kennedy's New Frontiersmen, Lyndon Johnson's Great Society warriors against poverty and injustice. Just as the Republican administrations of Richard Nixon, Gerald Ford, Ronald Reagan, and both Bushes had to contend with Democrats at all levels of the bureaucracy, post-Reagan Democratic administrations have to contend with anti-big-government conservatives at all levels.

Moreover, the world of think tanks and lobbying firms that beckon White House staffers and government officials when they finish their tenures is much more elaborate, thanks to the Reagan era. The rise of a conservative "counter-establishment" not only created a permanent Washington presence for Republicans, it also helped Democratic think tanks and lobbyists proliferate. Twenty-first-century Washington is filled with many more analysts, lawyers, government relations specialists, and retired bureaucrats hawking their ideas, pushing their agendas, shilling for their clients, than ever before.

Down Pennsylvania Avenue, on Capitol Hill, Congress and the Supreme Court have also been Reaganized. Although Reagan failed to get a conservative majority on the Court, since the 1980s the Court has been ever more conservative. Court decisions are more indulgent of state prerogatives, more skeptical about minority demands, more likely to side with the executive branch, and more suspicious of big government programs. The revolution resonates in the lower courts too, where many of the young men and women Reagan appointed became the senior judges. Of course, the judicial respect for precedent preserved much of the revolution Earl Warren's court began in the 1950s and 1960s. But, as in so many areas, the expansion of judicial prerogative that accelerated in the 1960s and 1970s has slowed, often to a crawl.

In Congress, the stylistic and substantive changes continue. Mimicking Reagan's communications revolution on the presidential level, members of the Congress and the Senate spend much more time playing to the cameras, consulting with spin doctors, perfecting their sound bites, and raising campaign dollars year round. Overall, they are also more responsive and more likely to rotate their offices than their predecessors were. Given modern celebrity politics' costs and pressures, many more Congress members and senators are millionaires or celebrities than in the 1960s and 1970s. Thanks to the great tensions between Republicans and Democrats over many Reagan agenda items, the parties are more polarized and many of these legislators are less likely to befriend members of the other party, let alone cooperate together.

All these Washington players are ever-conscious of playing in a world of 24/7 scrutiny, with an intrusive and ubiquitous media. These processes predated Reagan and were independent of him. But Reagan so mastered the media that he remains the gold standard in teaching politicians at all levels how to function. At the same time, Reagan and the conservative movement's assault on the media as automatically leftist has made the media and Americans—more conscious and defensive about the whole subject of media bias. In response, conservative talk show hosts began carrying the standard in the 1980s—often harshly—and Fox News emerged in 1996 as a populist, conservative counterbalance to CNN.

Even where Ronald Reagan did not necessarily inject a new policy or program, his era marked a turning point in so many realms. The fancy hotels and elaborately redesigned corporate offices lining a newly regenerated Pennsylvania Avenue were rooted in the 1980s. The palatial shopping malls dotting the city—and defining the suburbs—spread during the 1980s.

Within the corporate towers that rose in Washington and now ring the city, especially in suburban Virginia, the Reagan years still define many of the jobs and much of the corporate culture. Service jobs replaced manufacturing jobs. Security analysts and financial gurus proliferated as middle-class Americans plunged into the stock market. Since the 1980s, many of the most senior managers clock longer hours, African Americans and women enjoy wider acceptance, and the pressure to earn ever more to buy ever more has intensified.

Amid all the success stories, the misery of the walking wounded increased in the 1980s. Many of the discouraged Reagan Democrats, union members who lost their jobs through downsizing or company relocations after corporate raiders stripped assets and reconfigured businesses, often curse their one-time hero and regret their vote in 1980—and 1984. In Washington and many other American cities, along with the glorious rise of the black middle and upper classes, the underclass calcified. Millions of Americans, disproportionately black, remain mired in a multigenerational culture of poverty, deadened by drugs, revolving in and out of prison, left behind by the advances in technology and education.

Within the American home, in Washington and elsewhere, trends that shifted in the 1980s continue to affect many Americans' most intimate decisions. The rates of divorce, abortion, crime, illegitimate birth, drug use, and alcoholism, while still at epidemic levels, have started to level off or dip. Like Reagan himself, many more Americans are living much less conventional lives than their parents, yet nevertheless seek to resurrect their parents' traditional values. Some dismiss this as hypocrisy. Others appreciate what Reagan's secretary of education William Bennett called this "constructive hypocrisy," because at least seeking standards keeps humans grounded while somewhat slowing the rush toward new behaviors and lifestyle.

All in all, love him or hate him, Ronald Reagan's achievements were remarkable. One of the most mocked and underestimated men in American politics became the most influential president since Franklin Roosevelt. He cast an even longer shadow than his presidential record merits because he helped define an era, burning his brand on so many changes he did not specifically initiate or manage. His paradoxical era thus ends in another paradox. People will continue proclaiming the end of the Reagan Revolution—and it will be true—even as they will continue to live in a world shaped and defined by one of the twentieth century's most significant Americans, Ronald Wilson Reagan.

References

Chapter 1

2   "The American people...": Hamilton Jordan quoted in Austin Ranney, *The American Elections of 1980* (Washington, DC: American Enterprise Institute for Public Policy Research, 1981), 212.

7   "I'm a plain...": Ronald Reagan, "How to Make Yourself Important," *Photoplay* combined with *Movie Mirror*, Aug. 1942, 44.

10 "If you ask...": Laurence Leamer, "The First Couple," *Ladies' Home Journal*, Apr. 1983, 108.

10 "I *was* divorced...": Richard B. Stolley and Garry Clifford, "Ronald Reagan Opens Up: The President-Elect Talks About His Health, His Children and His Divorce," *People*, Dec. 29, 1981, 24.

14 "If Ronnie were...": *Newsweek*, Apr. 28, 1980, 33.

14 "Look, you know...": "Inside Ronald Reagan: A Reason Interview," *Reason*, July 1975, www.reason.com/news/show/29318.html.

14 "Maybe my party...": "Ronald Reagan to the Rescue!" *Esquire*, Feb. 1966, 1, 18.

15 "He's a lot...": *Newsweek*, Jan. 17, 1966, 31.

15 "the symbol...": Mrs. Hernando Courtright, quoted in "What 18 Smart Women Think of Ronald Reagan," *Good Housekeeping*, Jan. 1968, 153.

Chapter 2

29   "attempted to . . . ": Dwight D. Eisenhower to Edgar Newton Eisenhower, Nov. 8, 1954, in *The Papers of Dwight David Eisenhower*, vol. 15, ed. Louis Galambos and Daun Van Ee, doc. 1147. Available from the Dwight D. Eisenhower Memorial Commission, www.eisenhowermemorial.org/presidential-papers/first-term/documents/1147.cfm.

Chapter 3

48   "A conservative Strain . . . : Lee Hamilton to Tip O'Neill, Marginal District Survey, Mar. 6, 1980, Box 30, Series V: Party Leadership/Administrative Files, Thomas P. O'Neill Papers, John J. Burns Library, Boston College, Boston, MA.

48   "to consistently convert . . . ": Mickey Edwards to William Rusher, Jan. 31, 1978, 4, 8, Box 29:7, William A. Rusher MSS, Library of Congress, Washington, DC.

49   "What is being called pragmatism . . . ": *U.S. News & World Report*, May 5, 1980, 33.

49   "He gives you . . . ammunition": *Newsweek*, Apr. 21, 1980.

52   "negative views . . . ": *New York Times*, Nov. 16, 1980.

52   "This is . . . cosmic . . . ": *Newsweek*, Nov. 17, 1980.

Chapter 4

62   "think people are . . . ": William Safire, *Safire's New Political Dictionary* (New York, 1993) 220.

62   "cold, tough . . . ": Speaker's Press Conference, June 23, 1981, Box 11:1, Series VI: Press Relations; Speaker's Press Conference, July 16, 1981, Box 11:2, Series VI: Press Relations, both in Thomas P. O'Neill Papers, John J. Burns Library, Boston College, Boston, MA.

63   "seller": Ronald Reagan to Murray W. Ratzlaff, Dec. 14, 1983, 191892, Box 25, FG 001, Ronald Reagan Presidential Library, Simi Valley, CA.

65   "We have done . . . ": Ronald Reagan to Rep. Wendell Bailey, Sept. 9, 1981, OA 8618, Box 3, MB Oglesby Legislative Files, Margaret Tutweiler MSS, Reagan Library.

Chapter 5

71   "I do not...": Charles Manatt to Thomas P. O'Neill, Jan. 2, 1981, Box 4, Series II: Staff Files, Thomas P. O'Neill Papers, John J. Burns Library, Boston College, Brookline, MA.

73   "We are providing...": Ronald Reagan to Betty T. Benson, Madison, Alabama, Mar. 10, 1982, 065607, Box 2, Presidential Handwriting File, Ronald Reagan Presidential Library, Simi Valley, CA.

73   "how do we sustain...": Legislative Strategy Group Agenda, Jan. 27, 1983, CA 10972, Craig Fuller Files, Reagan Library.

74   "Yes, because for...": Dan Rather, "Ronald Reagan: Master Storyteller," *CBS News*, June 7, 2004. Available: www.cbsnews.com/stories/2004/06/07/48hours/main621459.shtml.

74   "spirit of bipartisanship...": Meeting with the bipartisan Budget Working Group, from Kenneth M. Duberstein, Ellen Bradley File, OA 13528, Reagan Library.

74   "original economic recovery...": "Conservative Leaders Denounce Reagan Tax Hike," July 20, 1982, OA 6387, Cons-Gen'l 1982 [4 of 6], Elizabeth H. Dole MSS, Reagan Library.

75   "the largest peacetime...": Newt Gingrich, Jack Kemp, et al. to Ronald Reagan, July 27, 1982, OA 8619, "Tax Bill 1982," MB Oglesby Legislative Files, Margaret Tutweiler MSS, Reagan Library.

76   "from 12.4% in...": "Indicators Up for 5th of Last 6 Months," Oct. 29, 1982, White House Talking Points, Dave's Project (2), OA14712, White House Office of Public Affairs, Reagan Library.

76   "Unemployment has little...": Richard S. Beal to Edwin Meese III, Strategic Evaluation Memorandum #8, Nov. 19, 1981, CFOA 465, Richard S. Beal MSS, Reagan Library.

76   The annual inflation...: "Inflation Continues Fall," Feb. 25, 1983, "Jobless Rate Continues Down in June; 1.1 Million New Jobs Created This Year," July 8, 1983, "Inflation Update," July 22, 1983, White House Talking Points, Dave's Project (2), OA14712, White House Office of Public Affairs, Reagan Library.

76   "quality of life...": Presidential Radio Address, Oct. 15, 1983.

78   "making sure we...": *Nation*, May 29, 1982: 648.

82   The working women...: Eleanor Smeal and Associates, "Maximizing the Women's Voice '84," 23, prepared for Democratic National Committee, Jan. 1984, Box 4 PR015 200446PD, Reagan Library.

83   "Me-Tarzan-You-Jane...: Ellen Goodman, quoted in James M. Wall, *Christian Century*, Aug. 31, 1983: 763.

83   "the end of...": Paul Boyer, ed., *Reagan as President: Contemporary Views of the Man, His Politics, and His Policies* (Chicago: Ivan R. Dee, 1990), 184.

84   "The Reagan Administration's environmental...": "White Paper—Environmental Policy," OA 11586, Environmental Information Program, Michael Deaver MSS, Reagan Library.

84   "more acreage...": Boyer, *Reagan as President*, 186.

84   "strengthened, rather than...": Ibid., 185.

Chapter 6

86   "Roses are red...": *U.S. News & World Report*, Dec. 7, 1981: 27.

87   "We've taken off...": Ronald Reagan, Remarks of the President to Eureka College Students and Faculty, February 6, 1984, 264871, Box 29, Folder 4/8, PR 016-04, Ronald Reagan Presidential Library, Simi Valley, CA.

88   "Our strength is...": Ronald Reagan, Address, East Room, White House, Public Papers, Jan. 16, 1984.

88   "what must be...": Ronald Reagan, handwritten insert to Draft, Presidential Address: Defense, March 22, 1983, 4, 133784SS, Reagan Library.

88   "The ideological struggle...": Ronald Reagan, radio address, Aug. 7, 1978, in Kiron K. Skinner, Annelise Anderson, and Martin Anderson, eds., *Reagan in His Own Hand* (New York: Simon & Schuster, 2001), 15, 13.

88   "neither an ec[onomic]...": Ronald Reagan, radio address, May 1975, in Skinner et al., *Reagan in His Own Hand*, 12.

89   "In our Hollywood....": Ronald Reagan to George Murphy, Dec. 9, 1986, in Kiron K. Skinner, Annelise Anderson, and Martin

Anderson, eds., *Reagan: A Life in Letters* (New York: Free Press, 2003), 470.

102   "Ronald Reagan hasn't....": *U.S. News & World Report*, June 6, 1988, 16.

103   "strategic review ... neither ... ": Carolyn McGiffert Ekedahl and Melvin Allan Goodman, *The Wars of Eduard Shevardnadze*, 2nd ed. (University Park: Pennsylvania State University Press, 1997), 119.

Chapter 7

106   "grew up in the small...": Ronald Reagan, written on "Memorandum for the President" from Anthony R. Dolan, Apr. 7, 1981, H0064, Box 1, Series II, 12/17/80–12/11/81, Folder 2 (3/19/81–5/31/81), Presidential Handwriting File, 1980–1989, Ronald Reagan Presidential Library.

107   "licks inflation ... ": Richard Nixon quoted in William F. Buckley Jr. to Ronald Reagan, Mar. 24, 1982, in William F. Buckley Jr., *The Reagan I Knew* (New York: Basic Books, 2008), 165.

113   In 1967 ... : *Fortune*, July 6, 1987, 26.

Chapter 8

126   "didn't say, 'well...": Michael Isikoff and David Corn, *Hubris: The Inside Story of Spin, Scandal and the Selling of the Iraq War* (New York: Crown, 2006), 20.

Further Reading

Chapter 1

Buckley, William F., Jr. *The Reagan I Knew*. New York: Basic Books, 2008.

Clifford, Clark. *Counsel to the President*. New York: Random House, 1991.

Edwards, Anne. *Early Reagan*. New York: Morrow, 1987.

Edwards, Lee. *The Conservative Revolution: The Movement That Remade America*. New York: Free Press, 1999.

Evans, Thomas W. *The Education of Ronald Reagan*. New York: Columbia University Press, 2006.

Reagan, Nancy. *My Turn: The Memoirs of Nancy Reagan*. New York: Random House, 1989.

Reagan, Ronald. *An American Life*. New York: Simon and Schuster, 1990.

Reagan, Ronald, and Richard C. Hubler. *Ronald Reagan Tells His Own Story: Where's the Rest of Me?* New York: Dell, 1965.

Troy, Gil. *Mr. and Mrs. President: From the Trumans to the Clintons*. Lawrence: University Press of Kansas, 2000.

Trudeau, G. B. *In Search of Reagan's Brain*. New York: Henry Holt, 1980, 1981.

Von Damm, Helen. *Sincerely, Ronald Reagan*. Ottawa, IL: Green Hill, 1976.

Wills, Garry. *New York Review of Books*, Dec. 20, 1990, 29.

——. *Reagan's America: Innocents at Home*. New York: Doubleday, 1986.

Chapter 2

Hamby, Alonzo. *Liberalism and Its Challengers: From F.D.R. to Bush*, 2nd ed. New York: Oxford University Press, 1992.

Hofstadter, Richard. *The American Political Tradition and the Men Who Made It*. New York: Random House, 1948.

Leuchtenburg, William. *Franklin D. Roosevelt and the New Deal*. New York: Harper Perennial, 1963.

Rossiter, Clinton. *Conservatism in America*. Cambridge, MA: Harvard University Press, 1982.

Sandel, Michael J. *Democracy's Discontent: America in Search of a Public Philosophy*. Cambridge, MA: Harvard University Press, 1996.

Wilentz, Sean. *The Rise of American Democracy*. New York: W. W. Norton, 2005.

Chapter 3

Clifford, Clark. *Counsel to the President: A Memoir*. New York: Random House, 1991.

Fortune, May 19, 1980.

Frum, David. *How We Got Here*. Lawrence: University Press of Kansas, 2004.

Huntington, Samuel. "The Democratic Distemper." In *The American Commonwealth 1976*, ed. Nathan Glazer and Irving Kristol. New York: Basic Books, 1976.

Jenkins, Philip. *Decade of Nightmares: The End of the Sixties and the Making of Eighties America*. New York: Oxford University Press, 2006.

Kirkpatrick, Jeane. "Dictatorships and Double Standards." *Commentary*. Nov. 1979.

Nation, May 1, 1980.

Schulman, Bruce. *The Seventies: The Great Shift in American Culture, Society and Politics*. New York: Free Press, 2001.

Skinner, Kiron K., Annelise Anderson, and Martin Anderson, eds. *Reagan, In His Own Hand*. New York: Free Press 2001.

Stockman, David A. *The Triumph of Politics: How the Reagan Revolution Failed*. New York: Harper and Row, 1986.

White, Theodore. *America in Search of Itself: The Making of the President 1956–1980*. New York: Warner Books, 1983.

Chapter 4

The Public Papers of President Ronald W. Reagan www.reagan.utexas. edu/archives/speeches/publicpapers.html.

Bell, Terrel H. *The Thirteenth Man: A Reagan Cabinet Memoir.* New York: Free Press, 1988.

Blumenthal, Sidney. *The Rise of the Counter-Establishment.* New York: Harper and Row, 1988.

Brinkley, Douglas, ed. *The Reagan Diaries.* New York: HarperCollins, 2007.

Cannon, Lou. *President Reagan: The Role of a Lifetime.* New York: Public Affairs, 1991, 2000.

Diggins, John Patrick. *Ronald Reagan: Fate, Freedom, and the Making of History.* New York: W. W. Norton, 2007.

Skinner, Kiron K., Annelise Anderson, and Martin Anderson, eds. *Reagan: A Life in Letters.* New York: Free Press, 2003.

Troy, Gil. *Morning in America: How Ronald Reagan Invented the 1980s.* Princeton, NJ: Princeton University Press, 2005.

Chapter 5

Collins, Robert M. *Transforming America: Politics and Culture during the Reagan Years.* New York: Columbia University Press, 2006.

Farrell, John A. *Tip O'Neill and the Democratic Century.* Boston: Little, Brown, 2001.

New Republic, Aug. 15, 1981.

O'Neill, Thomas P., with William Novak. *Man of the House: The Life and Political Memoirs of Speaker Tip O'Neill.* New York: Random House, 1987.

Schaller, Michael. *Right Turn: American Life in the Reagan–Bush Era, 1980–1992.* New York: Oxford University Press, 2007.

U.S. News & World Report, Aug. 20, 1984.

Wattenberg, Ben J. *The First Universal Nation: Leading Indicators and Ideas about the Surge of America in the 1990s.* New York: Free Press, 1991.

Chapter 6

Bush, George, and Brent Scowcroft. *A World Transformed.* New York: Knopf, 1998.

Dallek, Robert. *Ronald Reagan: The Politics of Symbolism*. Cambridge, MA: Harvard University Press, 1984.

FitzGerald, Frances. *Way Out There in the Blue: Reagan, Star Wars and the End of the Cold War*. New York: Simon and Schuster, 2000.

Gaddis, John Lewis. *The United States and the End of the Cold War: Implications, Reconsiderations, Provocations*. New York: Oxford University Press, 1992.

Matlock, Jack F., Jr. *Reagan and Gorbachev: How the Cold War Ended*. New York: Random House, 2004.

Newsweek, Dec. 21, 1987.

Schlesinger, James. "The Postwar Era: The Eagle and the Bear." *Foreign Affairs*, Summer 1985.

Schweizer, Peter. *Reagan's War: The Epic Story of His Forty Year Struggle and Final Triumph over Communism*. New York: Doubleday, 2002.

Chapter 7

Bellah, Robert N., et al. *Habits of the Heart: Individualism and Commitment in American Life*. Berkeley: University of California Press, 1985.

Brooks, Arthur C. *Who Really Cares: The Surprising Truth about Compassionate Conservatism*. New York: Basic Books, 2006.

Brownlee, W. Elliot, and Hugh Davis Graham, eds. *The Reagan Presidency: Pragmatic Conservatism and Its Legacies*. Lawrence: University Press of Kansas, 2003.

Hudson, Cheryl, and Gareth Davies, eds. *Ronald Reagan and the 1980s: Perceptions, Policies, Legacies*. New York: Palgrave Macmillan, 2008.

Sacks, Jonathan. *The Politics of Hope*. London: Vintage, 1997, 2000.

Chapter 8

Patterson, James T. *Restless Giant: The United States from Watergate to Bush v. Gore*. New York: Oxford University Press, 2005.

Troy, Gil. *Leading from the Center: Why Moderates Make the Best Presidents*. New York: Basic Books, 2008.

Wilentz, Sean. *The Age of Reagan: A History, 1974–2008*. New York: Harper, 2008.

Index

Index

Index